AN
English Spelling-Book

WITH

READING LESSONS

ADAPTED TO

THE CAPACITIES OF CHILDREN:

In Three Parts.

Calculated

TO ADVANCE THE LEARNERS

BY NATURAL AND EASY GRADATIONS;

And to teach

ORTHOGRAPHY AND PRONUNCIATION TOGETHER.

By *LINDLEY MURRAY*,

AUTHOR OF "AN ENGLISH GRAMMAR," &c. &c.

THE FORTY-SECOND EDITION.

YORK:

Printed by Thomas Wilson and Sons, High-Ousegate;
FOR LONGMAN, REES, ORME, BROWN, GREEN, AND
LONGMAN; FOR HARVEY AND DARTON, LONDON:
AND FOR WILSON AND SONS, YORK.
1834.

Price, bound, 1s. 6d.

INTRODUCTION.

The author of this manual, small as it is, did not commence the work, without a strong persuasion of the difficulties attending its execution. To form the threshold of learning, and accommodate instruction to the infant mind, both in matter and manner, has ever been deemed, by those who were capable of appreciating its nature and importance, an arduous and delicate work. On this ground, the author is sensible that the present performance is not without imperfections; but, as he flatters himself that it contains some improvements on the existing publications of a similar nature, he is imboldened to offer it for public inspection and decision.

A few observations on the plan and execution of the work, may be proper in this place, to give the reader a general idea of its nature and design. The use and advantage of many particular parts, are specified in the notes; which are chiefly designed for the teacher's attention.

The work is comprehended under three general divisions. One of the principal objects of the first part, is, to teach an accurate pronunciation of the elementary sounds. If this is effectually performed, in an early stage of learning, the child's future progress will be easy and pleasant: if it is then neglected, the omission will be rarely, if ever, completely supplied. To attain this important object, the author is persuaded that a considerable number of lessons, in monosyllables, is indispensable. No more of them are, however, admitted into his scheme, than are necessary to inculcate the various and exact sounds of the letters; each section being confined to a short exercise on a particular elementary sound. Many persons will probably think, as the author does, that if he had intended to teach only orthography, the monosyllabic lessons would not have been too numerous. Such words are easy and familiar to children; and they constitute the radical parts of the language. By hurrying the young pupil through this fundamental part of learning, he is often imperfectly taught, and eventually retarded in his progress.

The second part of the work affords the learner considerable aid, in pronunciation, as well as in orthography. The words of two syllables are not only classed in chapters, according to their accent, but they are arranged in sections, adapted to the sounds of the vowels and diphthongs, whether short, long, middle, or broad. Every section is also subdivided into smaller portions; in each of which all the words have the correspondent vowels and diphthongs sounded precisely alike. Words of three syllables would not admit of a classification so favourable to pronunciation. They are, however, arranged according to the length or shortness of their syllables; and this arrangement will facilitate the progress of learners, who would be perplexed and retarded by a constant recurrence of discordant sounds.

When the scholar has regularly passed through the first and second parts of the work, he will possess a considerable knowledge of the various powers of the letters; and will have acquired the habit of pronouncing accurately a great number and variety of common and useful words: he will then be well prepared for entering on the third part.

This part consists of words less familiar to children than those of the preceding parts; of rules for spelling and pronunciation; and of miscellaneous chapters, calculated to give the learner a radical knowledge, and diversified views, of the subject.

The reading lessons have been formed, or selected, with particular attention. The author has studied to simplify and adapt them to the capacity and taste of children; and to arrange them in natural and easy gradations: objects which he conceives to be of great importance. The infant capacity (as Quintilian justly observes) may be compared to a narrow-necked vessel, into which the liquor enters only by drops; and runs over, when either the quantity, or the quality, is not adapted to the entrance. Though a gradual rise in these lessons has been carefully observed, they will, it is presumed, be found to possess a considerable degree of simplicity throughout the book. To have given extracts from Addison, Blair, or Johnson, even at the end of the work, would have supposed that the child had, in the course of a few months, made a wonderful progress, both in his powers and experience.

All the narrative pieces in the book have the merit of being "True Stories." This, it is presumed, is no small recommendation. An ingenious author observes, that "It is an incentive to emulation to reflect, that 'what man has done, man may do.'" We add, that "what children have done, children may do;" and that probably a secret persuasion of the truth of this sentiment, is the ground of their preferring true stories to fictions.

The lessons of spelling, in every section, are illustrated by short appropriate reading lessons; which confirm the learner, step by step, in the pronunciation and orthography of the words he has repeated. These appropriate, as well as the promiscuous, reading lessons, through the book, contain no words which the child has not previously spelled, and which are not, therefore, familiar to him *. It is proper to observe, that some of the reading lessons are taken, either wholly or partly, from the writings of Barbauld; and a few, from those of Trimmer and Edgeworth.—The orthography of

---

* Except a few easy monosyllables, in the promiscuous reading lessons and a few participles, &c. whose primitives had been before exhibited.

Johnson, and the pronunciation of Walker, have been, almost universally, adopted in this work. They are authorities which few persons will be inclined to dispute.

When too much is attempted, but little is generally accomplished. The author has, on this principle, avoided the use of Italic letters, and all figures and marks, for the purpose of directing the pronunciation. They give the words and pages an uncouth appearance; and it may fairly be doubted whether they afford any real advantage to the pupil. The time spent in learning the use of these auxiliaries; the habit of depending entirely upon them; and the embarrassment on seeing the naked letters; may indeed, ultimately, render the expedient a disadvantage to the learner. After all the plans which ingenious persons have devised, to render the attainment of a good pronunciation easy to children, it must be allowed that much has not yet been accomplished. Perhaps, both the pronunciation and the orthography of words, can be no otherwise attained, than by a gradual acquisition of them individually, aided by a few general rules, and by classes of words analogically arranged.

INTRODUCTION.

This work is exhibited in a small, convenient size. The form is adapted both to the nature of the subject, and to the persons who are to use the book. The paper is fine, and the types are neatly formed, and very distinctly arranged. These are advantages superior, in the author's opinion, to the benefit supposed to be derived from the use of pictures. Children may, indeed, be amused by exhibitions of this nature; and, on some occasions, they are doubtless proper and useful: but they appear to be foreign to the business of a spelling-book; and probably divert the young attention from the first elements of learning, if they do not indispose it to a subject possessing so little comparative attraction.

If the work now offered to the public, should contribute to lighten the labours of teachers and pupils; and to cherish, in the infant mind, sentiments of piety and virtue, the author will not regret the time and pains he has spent in its composition. He will deem it an honour, to have smoothed, in any degree, the entrance to the temple of literature.

HOLDGATE, near YORK, 1804.

ADVERTISEMENT

to the FOURTH *edition.*

The FOURTH edition of this work has been considerably enlarged. The additions form twenty four pages of the book; and consist of many spelling, and some reading, lessons, a number of Exercises, and a few necessary explanations. The Exercises, which constitute the Appendix, exemplify the principles contained in various parts of the work. They are simple and easy; calculated to give the pupil a familiar knowledge of the subject; and to improve his powers of judgment and reflection.

The author hopes that the lessons in spelling, and in reading, will now be found fully adapted to each other, both in their nature and quantity; that the learner will be furnished with a proper and pleasing variety in his studies; and that, from the simplicity of the lessons, and the mutual aid they afford to one another, he will be gradually and effectually conducted to the art of reading with ease and propriety.

HOLDGATE, near YORK, 1805.

CONTENTS.

Part I.

The letters.—Easy monosyllables.—Correspondent reading lessons.

CHAP. 1. Lessons giving a general idea of the long, short, middle, and broad, sounds of the vowels and diphthongs 1
2. The short sounds of the vowels and diphthongs.......... 16
3. The long sounds of the vowels and diphthongs.......... 22
4. The middle sounds of the vowels and diphthongs........ 27
5. The broad sounds of the vowels and diphthongs.......... 29
6. Irregular sounds of the vowels........................ 31
7. Words containing consonants not sounded.............. 33
8. Consonants of different sounds....................... 36
9. Of the points or stops............................... 40
10. Promiscuous reading lessons......................... 41

Part II.

Easy words of two and three syllables.—Appropriate and promiscuous reading lessons.

CHAP. 1. Words of two syllables, with the accent on the first syllable.. 46
2. Words of two syllables, with the accent on the latter syllable... 60
3. Words of two syllables, which could not be conveniently arranged under either of the preceding chapters. 66
4. Promiscuous reading lessons.......................... 70
5. Words of three syllables. 83
6. Promiscuous reading lessons......................... 94

Part III.

Words less familiar to children—Correspondent reading lessons—Miscellaneous articles—Rules for spelling and pronunciation.

CHAP. 1. Words of three or more syllables................... 104
     2. Promiscuous reading lessons........................ 118
     3. Names of persons and places........................ 128
     4. Promiscuous reading lessons........................ 134
     5. Duties of children................................. 140
     6. Figures and numbers............................... 156
     7. Abbreviations used in writing and printing.......... 158
     8. Reading lessons in Italic, Old English, and Manuscript letters... 160
     9. Words exactly the same in sound but different in spelling and signification................................. 168
    10. Words which are often improperly confounded, in spelling or pronunciation, or both........................ 172
    11. Words spelled alike, but which differ in pronunciation and meaning....................................... 174
    12. Words in which the pronunciation differs remarkably from the spelling................................... 176
    13. Words which are often pronounced very erroneously..... 177
    14. Words in which certain terminations have exactly the same sound... 178
    15. Words in which the initial letters *e* and *i*, are often misapplied.. 180
    16. Explanation of vowels and consonants, syllables, accent, &c. 183
    17. The sounds of the letters............................ 189
    18. The silent letters.................................. 204
    19 Rules for spelling................................... 210
        Appendix.. 227

Part I.

The Letters—Easy monosyllables—Correspondent reading lessons.

Chapter 1.

Lessons giving a general idea of the long, short, middle, and broad sounds of the vowels and diphthongs.

Section 1.

The common alphabet—All the simple sounds of the language explained.

A B C D E F G H I
J K L M N O P Q R
S T U V W X Y Z

a b c d e f g h i
j k l m n o p q r
s t u v w x y z

The letters promiscuously disposed.

AV BR CD CO DO EF
HN IJ IL KR MW GC
OQ UV VY PB ST XZ

a s   b d   b p   c o   d p   e r
f l   h k   i j   i l   m n   m w
n u   p q   r t   v x   x z   g y

The vowels.

a   e   i   o   u, and sometimes w and y *

The consonants.

b c d f g h j k l m n p
q r s t v w x y z.

Double and triple letters.

ff   fi   ſh   ffi   fl   ffl

---

* W and Y are consonants, when they begin a word or syllable : in other situations, they are vowels.

The preceding alphabet, as it is commonly pronounced, does not contain all the simple elementary sounds of the English language. But as the learner should know them all, and be able to pronounce them with facility, it is necessary that the teacher inculcate them early, with the utmost care and exactness; otherwise the learner will probably never pronounce them perfectly. These elements are the foundation, on which the whole superstructure rests: the author has, therefore, arranged them in a distinct Table, (at pages 5 and 6,) which he has endeavoured to make as perspicuous as its importance demands.

The teacher should deliberately, and with great exactness, pronounce the words in this Table, and the child should repeat them after him, till they are tolerably well expressed. As the sounds only are, on this occasion, to be inculcated, it is not necessary that the learner should see the words, whilst he is repeating. The nature and use of the table should, however, be fully explained by the teacher, as soon as the scholar is able to comprehend the subject.

If the tutor think proper, he may, in teaching the original sounds to his young pupil, first express them simply, as they are denoted by the letters in the left-hand column; and afterwards as they are combined with other letters, in the words of the column on the right-hand. But the latter mode will be easier to the young voice; and will, perhaps in most cases, sufficiently answer the end in view. Of this, however, the tutor must judge. The instructer will often see the use of recurring to this table, to rectify the irregular pronunciation of children who have been taught the original sounds, in a defective or incorrect manner.

Several of the letters in the common alphabet, (which the child is supposed to have learned,) are not enumerated in the following Table; because they denote complex, not simple sounds; or because their sound is signified by other letters.

Table of the elementary sounds.

Letters denoting the simple sounds.			Words containing the simple sounds.
VOWELS.			
A long	as heard in		ale, day.
A short	as	in	mat, bat.
A middle	as	in	mar, bar.
A broad	as	in	all, daw.
E long	as	in	me, bee.
E short	as	in	met, net.
*I long	as	in	pine, pie.
I short	as	in	pin, tin.
O long	as	in	no, toe.
O short	as	in	not, lot.
O middle	as	in	move, moon.
*U long	as	in	mule, use.
U short	as	in	but, nut.
U middle	as	in	bull, full†.

---

* The long sounds of *i* and *u*, properly called diphthongal vowels, are, for convenience, inserted in the Table.

† For the various sounds which each of the preceding letters represents, see p. 31, and ch. 17, of Part III.

CONSONANTS.

B	as heard in	bat, tub.
D	as	in	dog, sod.
F	as	in	for, off.
V	as	in	van, love.
G	as	in	go, egg.
H	as	in	hop, ho.
K	as	in	kill, oak.
L	as	in	lap, tall.
M	as	in	my, mum.
N	as	in	nod, on.
P	as	in	pit, map.
R	as	in	rat, tar.
S	as	in	so, lass.
Z	as	in	zed, buzz.
T	as	in	top, hot.
W	as	in	wo, will.
Y	as	in	ye, yes.
NG	as	in	king, sing.
SH	as	in	shy, ash.
TH	as	in	thin, thick.
TH	as	in	then, them.
ZH	as	in	pleasure.

Some of the preceding elementary sounds are nearly related to one another. The young learner will, therefore, acquire a more accurate and distinct pronunciation of them, by frequently repeating words that contain those allied sounds. B and p, d and t, f and v, g and k, s and z, th and th, v and w, denote sounds in some degree similar. The careful expression of the following words, in quick succession, will effectually distinguish them. Here, the scholar, as in the former case, should attentively repeat after the teacher.

Sounds to be distinguished.

b from p   as in   bat, pat—sob, sop.
d from t   as in   dip, tip—mad, mat.
f from v   as in   fan, van—leaf, leave.
g from k   as in   gun, kin—dog, duck.
s from z   as in   sun, zed—kiss, buzz.
th from th   as in   thin, then—path, booth.
v from w   as in   vine, wine.

Section 2.

Syllables and words of two letters.

The vowel long.

ba	be	bi	bo	bu	by
ca	—	—	co	cu	—
da	de	di	do	du	dy
fa	fe	fi	fo	fu	fy
ga	—	—	go	gu	—

......

ha	he	hi	ho	hu	hy
ja	je	ji	jo	ju	—
la	le	li	lo	lu	ly
ma	me	mi	mo	mu	my
na	ne	ni	no	nu	ny

......

ra	re	ri	ro	ru	ry
sa	se	si	so	su	sy
ta	te	ti	to	tu	ty
va	ve	vi	vo	vu	vy

THE VOWELS AND DIPHTHONGS.

wa	we	wi	wo	—	—
ya	ye	yi	yo	yu	—
—	*ce	ci	—	—	cy
—	ge	gi	—	—	gy

The vowel generally short.

ab	eb	ib	ob	ub
ac	ec	ic	oc	uc
ad	ed	id	od	ud
af	ef	if	of	uf
ag	eg	ig	og	ug

......

ak	ek	ik	ok	uk
al	el	il	ol	ul
am	em	im	om	um
an	en	in	on	un
ap	ep	ip	op	up

---

* Ce, ci, cy, and ge, gi, gy, are placed at the end of this division, because the former are always pronounced soft; and the latter generally so.

ar	er	ir	or	ur
as	es	os	is	us
at	et	it	ot	ut
ax	ex	ix	ox	ux

Words of two letters.

The vowel generally long.

by	do	he	go	be
or	to	me	lo	ye
my	so	we	no	wo

The vowel short.

am	if	at	of	
an	in	it	on	us
as	is	up	ox	

Reading lesson.

Go up.	Is he up?	We do so.
Go in.	So am I.	Do so to us.
Go on.	Do go on.	Do as we do.

---

* When do, to, is, as, of, are used, not as syllables, but as words, they are pronounced doo, too, iz, az, ov.

THE VOWELS AND DIPHTHONGS.

Section 3.

Syllables and words of three letters, the position of the vowel varied*.

The vowel long.

bla	ble	bli	blo	blu	
bra	bre	bri	bro	bru	
cla	cle	cli	clo	clu	
cra	cre	cri	cro	cru	cry
dra	dre	dri	dro	dru	dry
fra	fre	fri	fro	fru	fry
gla	gle	gli	glo	glu	
gra	gre	gri	gro	gru	
pla	ple	pli	plo	plu	ply
pra	pre	pri	pro	pru	pry

* The syllables in this section form parts of a great number of words in the language, and afford much varied exercise to the organs of speech. They should, therefore, be repeated by the learner, till he is able to pronounce them with ease and distinctness.

sma	sme	smi	smo	smu	
sna	sne	sni	sno	snu	
spa	spe	spi	spo	spu	spy
the	thy	fly	shy	sky	try

The vowel generally short.

aft	eft	ift	oft	uft
alp	elp	ilp	olp	ulp
amp	emp	imp	omp	ump
and	end	ind	ond	und

......

ang	eng	ing	ong	ung
ank	enk	ink	onk	unk
ant	ent	int	ont	unt
apt	ept	ipt	opt	upt

......

arm	erm	irm	orm	urm
ask	esk	isk	osk	usk
ast	est	ist	ost	ust
add	egg	ill	odd	off
Ann	ass	ell	inn	

THE VOWELS AND DIPHTHONGS.

Reading lesson.

A fly.	An inn.	My arm.
An ant.	The ink.	An egg.
An ass.	The sky.	The end.

Go to Ann.   Go and ask.
She is ill.   By and by.
Is she up?   Try to do it.*

---

* "Children," says Dr. Beattie, "generally speak in short and separate sentences." Such sentences are therefore proper for their early lessons. They are adapted to their understandings, and calculated to prevent a drawling manner of expression. If children are taught to repeat, with correctness and fluency, the sentences contained in the First Part of this work, they will be much assisted in acquiring an accurate pronunciation. It is, however, proper to observe, that as every appropriate reading lesson is necessarily confined to the words contained in the same section, or in those which precede it, so limited a scope for invention would not admit of much taste or connexion, in selecting and arranging the sentences.

C

Section 4.

A sketch of the diphthongs *.

The principal diphthongs are;

ai	ea	ey	ou	ue
au	ee	oa	ow	ui
aw	ei	oi	oy	uy
ay	ew	oo	ua	

Some of these diphthongs have the sound of two vowels; some, of a single short vowel; some, of a single middle vowel; and others, of a single long or broad vowel.

1st. The sound of two vowels: as,

oi	in	boil;
oy	in	boy;
ou	in	our;
ow	in	cow.

---

* A sketch of the diphthongs is placed here, for the sake of order. The teacher will explain them to the learner, as soon as his progress will enable him to understand them.

2nd. The sound of a single short vowel: as,

ea in head   sounds   like e short;
ui in build   like i short;
ue in guest   like e short.

3d. The sound of a single middle vowel: as,

au in aunt   sounds   like middle a;
oo in cool   like middle o;
oo in good   like middle u.

4th. The sound of a single long or broad vowel; as,

ai in air   sounds   like a long;
ay in day   like a long;
ey in key   like e long;
au in daub   like a broad;
aw in paw   like a broad;
ow in slow   like o long.

Chapter 2.

The SHORT SOUNDS of the vowels and diphthongs.

Section 1.

Words of three letters.

a

bad	can	had	fat	mad	rag
bag	cap	has	lad	man	wag
bat	cat	hat	sad	mat	wax

e

bed	den	get	met	peg	red
beg	hen	leg	net	pen	vex
fed	men	let	set	pet	wet

i

bid	did	fig	him	lip	rid
big	dig	fin	his	pig	sit
bit	dim	fit	hid	pin	tin

o

box	fog	mop	pop	rob	sob
fox	hop	nod	pod	rod	sop
dog	hot	not	pot	rot	top

u

bud	cup	hum	mud	rub	sun
bun	cut	hug	mug	rug	sup
but	gun	hut	nut	run	tub

Reading lesson.

A pin.	The dog.	I had.
A cup.	The cat.	He has.
A top.	The pig.	We can.

A bad lad.   A red bud.
A mad dog.   A dry fig.
A fat pig.   A tin box.

He can dig.   It is hot.
I can hop.   Get my hat.
We can run.   Let us go.

Section 2.

Words of four letters.

a

band	glad	have	lass	sash
bank	flat	hand	fast	sand
damp	flax	land	last	span

e

bell	fret	nest	mend	tell
best	left	rest	send	well
desk	lent	west	sell	when

i

dish	hill	milk	sing	spin
fish	fill	mist	silk	swim
give	kiss	pink	ship	will
live	king	ring	skip	wish

o

blot	fond	gone	pond	soft
doll	frog	long	shop	spot
drop	from	lost	song	stop

u

burn	dust	jump	plum	spun
dull	hurt	lump	purr	sung
drum	hush	must	shut	tusk

Reading lesson.

A nest.   The king.   I wish.
A frog.   The ship.   I skip.
A pond.   The desk.   We jump.

A red spot.   Ring the bell.
A pink sash.   Shut the box.
The left hand.   Mend my pen.
A dish of fish.   Give me a pin.
A cup of milk.   Do not hurt me.

Section 3.

Words of five and six letters.

glass	shall	bless	fresh
grass	stamp	dress	shelf
plant	stand	flesh	shell
smell	bring	frisk	still
spell	brisk	spring	sting
spend	drink	stiff	string
cross	blush	crust	stung
tongs	brush	grunt	strut
strong	crush	snuff	trunk

Reading lesson.

A shell.   The grass.   I spell.
A brush.   The tongs.   He drinks.
A crust.   The shelf.   We stand.

A long string.   Brush my hat.
A strong man.   Bring the cup.
A brisk lad.   Drink the milk.

Section 4.

Words containing short diphthongs

e

dead	death	pearl	said
deaf	breath	tread	says
head	earth	spread	guess
bread	learn	thread	friend

i

| been | build | guilt | quill |

u

| blood | does | | young |
| flood | touch | | scourge |

Reading lesson.

The earth.   A deaf man.
My head.   A dead fly.
A friend.   A young frog.
I guess.   A crust of bread.
He said.   A bit of thread.
We learn.   A long quill.

Chapter 3.

The LONG sounds of the vowels and diphthongs.

Section 1.

Vowels and diphthongs like *a* in *ale*.

cake	face	haste	take
care	Jane	made	tape
gave	James	make	grape
air	clay	may	break
fair	day	maid	great
hail	hay	way	frail
tail	gain	play	snail
rain	gray	say	they
vain	hair	stay	their

Reading lesson.

It rains.　　　　　Take care.
It hails.　　　　　Make haste.

A long tail.　　　May I go?
A great cake.　　Stay by me.
A fair day.　　　Let us play.

THE VOWELS AND DIPHTHONGS.

Section 2.

Vowels and diphthongs like *e* in *me*.

Eve	she	here	these
ear	read	steal	week
eat	bleat	wheat	geese
east	clean	bee	green
pea	mean	see	sheep
tea	leave	feed	sleep
dear	sheaf	feet	sweet
fear	shear	keep	sleeve
leaf	speak	tree	field
neat	squeak	weed	piece

Reading lesson.

A green field.   The sheep bleat.
A sweet pea.   The pigs squeak.
A sheaf of wheat.   Here is a bee.
A piece of bread.   Feed the geese.
A cup of tea.   Eat the grapes.

LONG SOUNDS OF

Section 3.

Vowels and diphthongs like *i* in *pine*.

Ice	kind	nice	blind
bite	kite	rice	wipe
dine	like	ripe	shine
fine	mice	side	smile
fire	mild	time	quite
line	mind	wine	spice

die	pie	tie	buy
lie	rie	vie	eye

Reading lesson.

A sweet smile.   The sun shines.
A nice pie.   It is a fine day.
A ripe plum.   Bring the line.
A glass of wine. Fly the kite.
A blind man.   It is time to read.
A kind friend.   I like to read.

Section 4.

Vowels and diphthongs like *o* in *no*.

old	home	roll	bone
cold	hope	rose	stone
gold	mole	told	smoke
hold	most	tone	stroke

coat	cloak	low	grow
load	toast	mow	show
road	door	blow	snow
roar	floor	crow	sew

Reading lesson.

A hot roll.
A red cloak.
A sweet rose.
A load of hay.
A bad road.
A clean floor.

Shut the door.
The fire smokes.
It is a cold day.
It snows fast.
Bring my coat.
Let us go home.

Section 5.

Vowels and diphthongs like *u* **in** *mule.*

use	fume	mute	tube
cure	lute	pure	tune
duke	mule	puke	plume
cue	dew	new	slew
due	clew	pew	ewe
hue	few	blew	lieu
blue	mew	flew	view

Reading lesson.

The sky is blue.   In a few weeks, I hope
The cat mews.   to read well.
The mule frisks.   I will make the best
The new road.   use of my time.

Chapter 4.

The MIDDLE sounds of the vowels and diphthongs*.

Like *a* in *bar*.

are	cart	harm	part
art	card	lark	tart
bark	far	large	sharp
dark	hard	star	smart
ha	jaunt	heart	launch
aunt	guard	hearth	haunch

Like *o* in *move*.

lose	prove	whom	do
move	who	whose	Rome
coo	noon	broom	shoe
cool	poor	goose	you

---

* We have found it convenient to arrange the *o* in *move*, amongst the middle sounds of the vowels: and as its sound is longer than *o* in *not*, and rather shorter than *o* in *no*, we presume the arrangement is allowable.

MIDDLE SOUNDS OF

too	root	shoot	true
food	room	spoon	fruit
moon	soon	stool	your

Like *u* in *bull*.

| bush | full | puss | bull |
| push | pull | put | |

book*	look	good	foot
cook	rook	hood	wood
hook	took	stood	wool

Reading lesson.

Good fruit. The full moon.
A fat goose. The dog barks.
A poor rook. The bull roars.
A dark room. Puss purrs.

I hurt my foot. Put by the stool.
I lost my shoe. Do not push me.
Is it true? Whose book is it?
Who said so? I shall soon learn
Look at me. to spell.

* In the pronunciation given to these words, the author is supported by Nares, Sheridan, and the practice of the best speakers.

Chapter 5.

The BROAD sounds of the vowels and diphthongs *.

Section 1.

Vowels and diphthongs like *a* in *all*.

ball	tall	warm	scald
call	wall	wart	small
fall	salt	false	swarm
daub	daw	claw	shawl
fault	paw	draw	straw
gauze	raw	lawn	broad
caw	saw	crawl	George

Reading lesson.

A soft ball.　　　　A straw hat.
A broad band.　　　A tall man.
A gauze cap.　　　　A warm shawl.

The rooks caw.　　　The snow falls.
The snails crawl.　　My ball is lost.
Puss has sharp claws.　Who calls me?

---

* Vowels and diphthongs are called *broad*, when they take the sound of broad *a*, or are proper diphthongs.

Section 2.

Proper diphthongs, in which both the vowels are sounded: *oi* and *oy*, as in *boy*; *ou* and *ow*, as in *cow*.

oil	joy	thou	ground
boil	toy	cloud	cow
moist	our	found	how
noise	out	house	now
spoil	loud	mouse	owl
voice	shout	pound	growl
boy	sour	round	down
coy	flour	sound	gown

Reading lesson.

How do you do?
Sit down. Read to me.
Now leave your books.
Do not make a noise.
Owls fly in the dark.
Moles live in the ground.

Chapter 6.

Words in which the vowels deviate from the sounds they have in the scale at page 5*.

A like *o* short.

was	wash	want
wast	wasp	what

I like *u* short.

dirt	flirt	first	bird
shirt	spirt	stir	squirt

I like *e* short.

birth	firm	girl	skirt
mirth	gird	girt	whirl

O like *u* short.

come	glove	some	work
done	love	son	worm
dove	none	word	world

---

* These sounds of the vowels, so different from the regular sounds of them in the scale, have been reserved for a distinct appropriate chapter; that the young learner might not be perplexed with the various and discordant powers of the vowels blended together.

IRREGULAR SOUNDS OF

O like *a* broad.

cord	fork	born	for
lord	horse	corn	nor
cork	storm	horn	short

U like middle *o*.

crude	rule	prude	truce
rude	brute	prune	spruce

| *There | where | yes | her |

Reading lesson.

Has Ann done her work?
Yes she has.
She is a good girl.   I love her.
I have been ill.   Come to me.
Give me some drink.
I love to learn.   Where is my book?
What shall I read?

---

* *E* sounds like long *a* in *there, where;* like short *i* in *yes;* and like short *u* in *her.*

Chapter 7.

Words containing consonants not sounded.

Section 1.

Words with silent consonants, the vowel or diphthong having the short or the middle sound.

b silent	k	cock	half
lamb	back	clock	calm
limb	black	mock	could
dumb	quack	duck	should
thumb	neck	knit	would
crumb	pick	knot	w
g	sick	knock	wrap
gnat	trick	l	wrist
gnash	quick	calf	wrong

Reading lesson.

A fat calf.
A hard knot.
The ducks quack.
The cock crows.
The gnats bite.

Pick up the crumbs.
Who knocks at the door?
Ann should learn to knit and sew.

Section 2.

Words with silent consonants, the vowel or diphthong having the long or the broad sound.

b silent	knead	fight	bought
climb	l	light	ought
comb	talk	might	thought
g	walk	night	bough
sign	stalk	sight	plough
reign	yolk	thigh	dough
gnaw	folks	eight	though
k	gh	neigh	w
knife	high	straight	write
know	sigh	caught	wrote
knee	bright	taught	sword

SILENT CONSONANTS.

Reading lesson.

A new comb.
A sharp knife.
A high wall.
A fine sight.

A bright star.
A light night.
The horse neighs.
The dogs fight.

The bough of a tree.
The stalk of a rose.
The yolk of an egg.
Dogs gnaw bones.
Jane kneads the dough.
George ploughs the field.

Puss can climb trees.
I know how to read.
I wish I could write.
Come let us walk.
What o'clock is it?
It is eight o'clock.
I thought so.

Chapter 8.

Consonants, single and double, which have different sounds.

Section 1.

Single consonants.

c hard like *k*.

cash	crum	clash	scar
crab	curd	cling	scum
cane	cold	creep	count
call	cool	crawl	crown

c soft like *s*.

dance	pence	since	hence
dunce	fence	prince	whence
lace	nice	cease	juice
place	price	piece	voice

g hard.

glad	gasp	glass	grand
grin	gust	grass	grunt

g soft.

gem	gin	age	hedge

CONSONANTS OF DIFFERENT SOUNDS.

s sharp.

sand	dress	bricks	nurse
send	gloss	tricks	purse
seed	haste	goose	seat
side	waste	straw	sweet

s flat like *z*.

his	rags	birds	beds
hers	ribs	doves	heads
keys	hares	pears	please
tease	wares	praise	croaks

Reading lesson.

Jane has made a nice plum tart.

Take a piece of it.

George gave me a book.

I am glad I can read it.

I hope I shall not be a dunce.

Bricks are made of clay.

Glass is made of sand.

Wine is the juice of grapes.

E

Section 2.

Double consonants.

th sharp.

thank	thick	breath	cloth
think	thin	health	thing
three	throw	teeth	north
throne	throat	mouth	south

th flat.

than	this	that	baths
then	thus	them	paths
they	these	thy	clothes
theirs	those	thine	smooth

ch like *tch*.

Charles	chin	much	rich
charge	chick	such	which
chair	cheese	coach	peach
child	choice	couch	reach

ch like *sh*.

inch	bench	tench	French
pinch	bunch	stench	chaise

CONSONANTS OF DIFFERENT SOUNDS.

ch like *k*.

| chart | chasm | scheme | school |

gh and *ph* like *f*.

| rough | cough | phiz | nymph |
| tough | laugh | phrase | soph |

Reading lesson.

Clean your teeth.
Wash your mouths.
Then your breath will be sweet.
Do not throw stones.
Come in.
Reach a chair.
Take some bread and cheese.

Who gave you these pears?
James gave them to us.
Thank him for them.
I have a fine peach, and a bunch of grapes.
I will give you some of them. *

---

* See, at page 237, the observations on the propriety of the learner's spelling the appropriate reading lessons, as exercises off the book.

Chapter 9.

Of the points and notes used in composing sentences.

A comma is marked............ thus ,
A semicolon..................... thus ;
A colon........................... thus :
A period, or full stop.......... thus .
A note of interrogation........ thus ?
A note of admiration........... thus !
A parenthesis..................... thus (

Pauses in reading.

The learner should stop,

at the comma,   till he could count.. one ;
at the semicolon, till..................... two ;
at the colon,   till .... three ;
at the period,   till .... four.

Chapter 10.

Promiscuou sreading lessons.

Section 1.

Breakfast.

The sun shines.

It is time to get up.

Jane, come and dress Charles.

Wash his face, and neck, and make him quite clean.

Comb his hair. Tie his frock.

Now, Charles, we will go down stairs.

Fetch that stool. Sit down.

Here is some milk; and here is a piece of bread.

Do not spill the milk.

Hold the spoon in the right hand.

This is the right hand.

The crust is hard: do not leave it; sop it in the milk.

Do not throw the bread on the floor.

We should eat bread, and not waste it.

There is a poor fly in the milk.

Take it out. Put it on this dry cloth. Poor thing! It is not quite dead. It moves; it shakes its wings; it wants to dry them: see how it wipes them with its feet.

Put the fly on the floor, where the sun shines.

Then it will be dry and warm.

Poor fly! I am glad it was not dead.

I hope it will soon be well.

Section 2.

Puss.

Where is puss?

There she is.

Do not pull her by the tail: that will hurt her.

Charles does not like to be hurt: and puss does not like to be hurt.

I saw a boy hurt a poor cat; he took hold

of her tail: so she put out her sharp claws, and made his hand bleed.

Stroke poor puss.

Give her some milk.

Puss likes milk.

Now that Charles is so kind to her, she will not scratch, nor bite him.

She purrs, and looks glad.

Section 3.

Reading.

Come to me, Charles. Come and read.

Here is a new book.

Take care not to tear it.

Good boys do not spoil their books.

Speak plain.

Take pains, and try to read well.

Stand still.

Do not read so fast.

Mind the stops.

What stop is that?

It is a full stop.

Charles has read a whole page now.
This is a page.   This is a leaf.
A page is one side of a leaf.
Shut the book.   Put it by.
Now give me a kiss.

Section 4.

Rain.

Shall we walk?

No; not now.   I think it will rain soon.

Look how black the sky is!

Now it rains!   How fast it rains!

Rain comes from the clouds.

The ducks love rain.

Ducks swim, and geese swim.

Can Charles swim?

No.   Charles is not a duck, nor a goose: so he must take care not to go too near the pond, lest he should fall in.   I do not know that we could get him out: if we could not, he would die.

When Charles is as big as James, he shall learn to swim.

Section 5.

A walk.

It does not rain now.

The sky is blue.

Let us take a walk in the fields; and see the sheep, and the lambs, and the cows, and trees, and birds.

Call Tray. He shall go with us.

He wags his tail. He is glad to see us, and to go with us.

Stroke poor Tray.

Tray likes those who stroke him, and feed him, and are kind to him.

Do not walk on the grass now. It is too high; and it is quite wet.

Walk in this smooth, dry path.

There is a worm. Do not tread on it.

Can Charles climb that high stile?

O what a large field!

This is not green. It is not grass.

No; it is corn. It will be ripe soon.

Bread is made of corn. I dare say Charles does not know how bread is made. Well, some time I will tell him.

Now let us go home.

Shall we look at the bees in their glass hive?

Will the bees sting us?

No; they will not sting us, if we do not tease, nor hurt them.

Wasps will not sting us, if we do not hurt them.

There is a wasp on my arm.

Now it is gone.

It has not stung me.

Section 6.

Dinner.

The clock strikes.

It is time to go in, and dine.

Is the cloth laid?

Where are the knives, and forks, and plates?

Call Ann.

Are your hands clean?

Sit down.

Do not take the broth yet; it is too hot: wait till it is cool.

Will you have some lamb, and some peas?

Do not smack your lips, or make a noise, when you eat.

Take some bread. Break the bread: do not bite it.

I do not put the knife in my mouth, for fear I should hurt my lips. Knives are sharp: they are to cut with, and not to put in one's mouth, or to play with.

Jane must shake the cloth out of doors.

The birds will pick up the crumbs.

Now let us go and play with George.

Section 7.

The poor blind man.

There is a poor blind man at the door.

He is quite blind. He does not see the sky, nor the ground, nor the trees, nor men.

He does not see us, though we are so near him. A boy leads him from door to door.

Poor man!

O it is a sad thing to be blind!

We will give the blind man some bread and cheese.

Now he is gone.

He is a great way off.

Poor blind man!

Come in, Charles. Shut the door.

I wish the poor blind man had a warm house to live in, and kind friends to take care of him, and to teach him to work. Then he would not beg from door to door.

Part II.

Easy words of two and three syllables. Appropriate and promiscuous reading lessons *.

Chapter 1.

Words of two syllables, with the accent on the first syllable †.

Section 1.

Both the syllables short.

Ab sent	pack thread	branch es
ac cent	Nap kin	cab bage
bad ness	ac tive	pas sage
flan nel	bas ket	stand ing
gra vel	blan ket	rag ged

---

* The words of two syllables are arranged in small divisions under each section. Every word, in each of these subdivisions, has the correspondent vowels or diphthongs, in both the syllables, sounded exactly alike. The leading word which determines the pronunciation of the class to which it belongs, is distinguished by a capital letter.

If nothing more were gained, by the peculiar arrangement of words in this part of the work, than the aid which words so classed together afford, in teaching and learning to spell, it would be an object of considerable importance.

† See the rules for dividing syllables, Part III. Chapter 19, page 210.

ACCENT ON

Mat ter	ver mine	chil dren
af ter	Chest nut	cyg net
an ger	beg gar	Shil ling
an swer	bet ter	build ing
back wards	en ter	ci vil
chap ter	e ver	chick en
chat ter	fea ther	fi nish
da mask	le mon	kit chen
ga ther	let ter	li nen
lad der	me lon	mis chief
ra ther	ne ver	sing ing
sam pler	pep per	swim ming
Bel man	sel dom	ti mid
break fast	Shep herd	wick ed
phea sant	tem per	Hic kup
plea sant	ten der	bit ter
ser vant	wea ther	din ner
Bless ing	Brick bat	fil bert
cer tain	dis tance	fin ger
hed ges	in fant	ri ver
learn ing	in stant	scis sors
self ish	Ill ness	sil ver
ser vice	in sect	sis ter
whet ting	in step	twit ter

THE FIRST SYLLABLE.

whi ther	Con duct	Mur mur
win ter	blos som	bro ther
Cob web	cob bler	co lour
know ledge	com mon	com fort
non sense	doc tor	flut ter
ob ject	pro per	fur ther
Bob bin	pros per	huck ster
gos ling	scho lar	hus band
bon net	Mus lin	mo ther
cot tage	cur tain	num ber
o live	no thing	o ther
o range	nurs es	puck er
pro mise	pu nish	sto mach
quar rel	some thing	suf fer
ro bin	sul len	sum mer
stock ings	tur nip	sup per
squat ting	wor ship	thun der

Reading lesson.

A basket of figs.
A fine melon.
Pleasant weather.
Good children.
A cold winter.
A warm cottage.

A huckster sells fruit and cakes.
A cobbler mends shoes.
Linen is made of flax.

Section 2.

Both the syllables long*.

Ba by	scarce ly	lea ky
dai ly	va ry	mea ly
dain ty	Hail stone	neat ly
dai ry	may pole	nee dy
dai sy	rain bow	slee py
fair ly	sa go	sweet ly
hai ry	scare crow	wea ry
ha sty	where fore	Kind ly
gra vy	Clear ly	bright ly
la dy	dear ly	fine ly
late ly	drea ry .	high ly
la zy	ea sy	i vy
pa stry	fee bly	like ly
rai ny	gree dy	live ly
safe ly	grea sy	migh ty

---

* It is proper, in this place, to observe, that the long and the short vowels, have degrees in their length and shortness. If, therefore, the vowels classed as long ones, in many of the syllables, should not be deemed so long as they are in other circumstances, they may nevertheless be properly considered as specific long vowels. In a work

mi ry	low ly	sto ry
spi cy	most ly	whol ly
ti dy	no bly	Beau ty
ti ny	on ly	du ty
Bo ny	po ny	du ly
cro ny	poul try	fu ry
glo ry	ro sy	new ly
ho ly	slow ly	pure ly
home ly	smo ky	sure ly

Reading lesson.

A sweet baby.
A tidy girl.
A dairy maid.
A lazy boy.
A rainy day.
A long story.

Charles is a lively boy.
The rainbow has fine colours.
The robin sings sweetly.

---

of this kind, it would perplex instead of informing the learner, if the several variations in the long and the short sounds, were designated. The situation of the accent will, in most cases, direct the learner, as to the precise length which every long vowel should have.

Section 3.

The first syllable short, the second long.

Al ley	mea dow	Bor row
an gry	yel low	fol low
car ry	there fore	hol low
hap py	Sil ly	swal low
Mer ry	fil thy	Tur key
cher ry	pi ty	dus ky
ve ry	pret ty	fur ry
a ny	quick ly	hun gry
ma ny	Pil low	sul try
en vy	prim rose	stu dy
plen ty	wi dow	ug ly
ear ly	win dow	ho ney
hea vy	Bo dy	mo ney
rea dy	cof fee	mon key
Bel low	co py	coun try
fel low	sor ry	jour ney

Reading lesson.

The bull bellows.
The monkey chatters.
The swallows twitter.
The turkey struts.

Bees make wax and honey.
How sweet the meadows smell.

Section 4.

The first syllable long, the second short.

Blame less	peel ing	vi al
care less	pier cing	wi ser
pa rent	Fe ver	Cro cus
pave ment	read er	glow worm
Pa per	reap er	old er
dra per	ei ther	o ver
fa vour	nei ther	whole some
neigh bour	Blind ness	Pew ter
tai lor	bright ness	hu mour
Feel ing	kind ness	tu mour
be ing	qui et	tu tor
creep ing	si lent	Mu sic
hear ing	Li on	fu el
freez es	bri er	gru el
glean ing	ti ger	jew el
mean ing	tire some	stu pid

Reading lesson.

The lion roars.

The tiger growls.

Paper is made of rags.

Tailors make clothes.

Drapers sell cloth.

ACCENT ON

Section 5.

The middle sounds of the vowels and diphthongs.

The second syllable short.

Art less	car pet	mas ter
dark ness	far thing	par lour
harm less	mar ket	Fool ish
har vest	par tridge	bloom ing
scar let	spark ling	choos es
Charm ing	Fa ther	stoop ing
arch ing	gar ter	do ing
card ing	lar ger	cru el

The second syllable long.

Ar my	Gloo my	Bul ly
bar ley	roo my	ful ly
par sley	smooth ly	pul ley
part ly	ru by	woo dy
laun dry	rude ly	wool ly

Reading lesson.

A field of barley.   A kind master.
A fine harvest.   A good father.
A charming walk.   A blooming boy.
A green carpet.   A foolish trick.

Section 6.

The broad sounds of the vowels and diphthongs*.

The second syllable short.

Wal nut	wa ter	moun tain
al ter	warm er	tow el
au tumn	or der	Count er
daugh ter	or chard	floun der
draw er	Cow slip	flow er
hal ter	clown ish	show er
sau cer	foun tain	cow ard

The second syllable long.

Gau dy	sau cy	Boun ty
haugh ty	for ty	clou dy
naugh ty	lord ly	drow sy
pal try	stor my	proud ly

Reading lesson.

A cup and saucer.
A pretty flower.
A cloudy day.
A naughty boy.
Get some cowslips.
Water the plants.
A mountain is a very high hill.

---

* Vowels and diphthongs are called *broad*, when they take the sound of broad *a*, or are *proper* diphthongs.

Section 7.

Words in which the vowel of the latter syllable is mute, or scarcely perceptible.

The first vowel short.

Ap ple*	per son	Bot tle
an cle	hea ven	coc kle
cac kle	rec kon	gob ble
can dle	Lit tle	cot ton
daz zle	kin dle	oft en
han dle	gi ven	soft en
fas ten	lis ten	Buc kle
hap pen	pri son	bun dle
rat tle	mid dle	crum ble
Gen tle	nim ble	dou ble
ket tle	sic kle	do zen
les son	sin gle	glut ton
med dle	thim ble	pur ple
net tle	whis tle	sho vel
peb ble	wrin kle	trou ble

---

* Apple, happen, &c. should be pronounced as if they were written, ap pl, hap pn.

The first vowel long.

A ble	Nee dle	fright en
ba con	ea gle	light en
ba sin	e ven	ri pen
cra dle	e vil	i dle
fa ble	peo ple	tri fle
ma son	rea son	No ble
ta ken	sea son	bro ken
rai sin	stee ple	cho sen
ra ven	trea cle	fro zen
sta ble	Bi ble	o pen
ta ble	bri dle	wo ven

Reading lesson.

An idle girl.
A nimble boy.
A little child.
A black pebble.
A sweet apple.
A double daisy.

The goose cackles.
The turkey gobbles.
The raven croaks.
Open the door.
Snuff the candles.
Do not trouble me.

Chapter 2.

Words of two syllables, with the accent on the latter syllable.

Section 1.
Both the syllables short.

At tend	ex pect	in struct
a mend	neg lect	in trust
at tempt	per verse	Con fess
la ment	them selves	con sent
a gain	Dis tress	con tent
a gainst	him self	of fence
Ab surd	it self	pos sess
af front	in tend	Sub mit
a mong	in vent	un fit
a mongst	Dis turb	un til
Ex cel	in dulge	un twist

Reading lesson.

When you have done wrong, confess it.

Try to excel others in learning.

Do not affront me.

Be content with what you have.

Attend to what the master says.

Do not disturb us.

Section 2.

Both the syllables long.

Be have	de ceive	Be fore
de clare	re ceive	be hold
pre pare	re peat	be low
re late	Be hind	re pose
de lay	be sides	re store
re frain	de light	Mo rose
re main	di vide	pro pose
Se rene	de ny	pro voke
se vere	de sig	De mure
be lieve	de sire	pre sume
be tween	re mind	re buke
de ceit	re quire	re fuse

Reading lesson.

Behave well.
Think before you speak.
Do as your parents desire you to do.
Repeat your lesson.
Do not provoke any body.
Deceive no one.
A good boy delights his friends.

G

ACCENT ON

The first syllable short, the second long.

A wake	ac cuse	sin cere
ac quaint	a muse	Dis like
a fraid	tra duce	dis guise
a way	Em brace	in cline
Ad mire	ex plain	in quire
a live	main tain	in vite
a rise	per suade	Un kind
ar rive	Dis grace	un ripe
man kind	mis take	un tie
A dore	dis dain	sur prise
a go	mis laid	Sup pose
af ford	Dis creet	sup port
a lone	dis please	un bolt
A buse	in deed	un known

Reading lesson.

Unripe fruit is not wholesome.

Awake, it is time to get up.

If the dog barks, be not afraid.

Bees will not sting us, if we let them alone.

Go away now, but come again.

Be sincere in all you say or do.

Section 4.

The first syllable long, the second short.

De camp	pre tend	be yond
re pass	pre vent	re solve
re past	re fresh	re volve
se dan	re gret	Re turn
De fend	re spect	be come
de pend	re quest	e nough
de serve	Be gin	pre judge
di rect	de sist	Fo ment
di vert	re sist	fore tell
pre fer	re build	pro fess
pre serve	Be long	pro tect

Reading lesson.

Come, begin your work.
Go on. Now you have done enough.
To whom does this book belong?
To Charles. He lent it to us.
We must return it to him.
James is not well.
We must try to divert him.
He deserves favour.
I respect and love him.

Section 5.

The middle sounds of the vowels and diphthongs.

The first syllable short:

A larm	ap prove	Dis prove
a part	ba boon	im prove
Dis arm	bal loon	in trude
dis card	dra goon	Buf foon
Em bark	rac koon	un do
en large	shal loon	un truth

The first syllable long.

De part	Re move
be calm	be hoove
re gard	re prove
re mark	re cruit

Reading lesson.

The work is ill done: undo it.
Try to improve.
Never tell an untruth.
To depart, is to go away from a place.
To embark, means to enter a ship.

Section 6.

The broad sounds of the vowels and diphthongs.

The first syllable short.

A dorn	In form	ac counts
ab hor	mis call	a loud
a broad	with draw	al low
ap plaud	A noint	a round
Ex hort	ap point	En joy
ex tort	a void	em ploy
per form	A bout	em broil

The first syllable long.

Be cause	De coy	De vour
de fraud	de stroy	de vout
de form	re coil	re nounce
re call	re joice	re nown
re ward	re join	re sound

Reading lesson.

That boy is happy, because he is good.

He performs his work quickly and well.

Shall we go abroad to day?

Read aloud, but not too loud.

Take care to avoid a singing tone.

Do not miscall the words.

Chapter 3.

Dissyllables which could not conveniently be arranged under either of the preceding chapters *.

Section 1.

Containing a number of them differently accented.

Accent on the first syllable.

Can not	bot tom	fear ful
rag man	sor row	fe male
thank ful	cur rants	cry ing
spar row	hunts man	i ron
emp ty	some times	light ning
help less	up per	li lach
lei sure	ut most	ri ses
plea sure	work house	wri ting
sen tence	care ful	mo ment
chil blain	grateful	mourn ful
in to	ta king	no tice
wis dom	crea ture	ro ses
wo men	cheer ful	use ful

---

* The words in this chapter could not be omitted, as they are contained in the subsequent reading lessons. They are arranged with as much regard to pronunciation, as their variety would admit.

IRREGULAR WORDS.

gar den	wo man	hors es
par don	wor sted	scorch es
spar kle	al most	tor ture
bush es	al so	talk ing
cuc koo	al ways	walk ing
look ing	fall en	hous es
pud ding	for tune	out side
su gar	for wards	loi ter
wood en	morn ing	noi sy

Accent on the second syllable.

as sist	up on	o blige
fa tigue	un less	o bey
com mand	pur sue	pro vide
con fine	per haps	for give
in crease	her self	for get
with in	be come	our selves
with out	fire side	your selves

Reading lesson.

I love to hear the cuckoo.
How sweet the garden smells!
Lilachs are pretty trees.
Roses are very sweet.
My parents provide many things for me.
I should always be grateful to them.
I will obey their commands.

IRREGULAR WORDS.

Section 2.

Containing words ending in *ed*.

1st. Such as are pronounced as one syllable.

d having its usual sound.

beg ged	lov ed	pleas ed
swell ed	rub bed	seal ed
fledg ed	scrub bed	seem ed
kill ed	pray ed	bri bed
liv ed	rais ed	ti red
mov ed	sa ved	mow ed
prov ed	call ed	show ed
crown ed	warm ed	mu sed
drown ed	form ed	u sed

d sounded like *t*.

ask ed	fix ed	nurs ed
hatch ed	mix ed	work ed
scratch ed	miss ed	pla ced
thatch ed	wish ed	ra ked
thrash ed	whip ped	scorch ed
dress ed	cross ed	talk ed
press ed	drop ped	reach ed
perch ed	hop ped	preach ed
stretch ed	lock ed	crouch ed

IRREGULAR WORDS.

2d. Such as are pronounced as two syllables *.

dread ed	ha ted	fold ed
mend ed	sha ded	load ed
tempt ed	tast ed	mould ed
gild ed	wait ed	roast ed
sift ed	wast ed	scold ed
last ed	feast ed	count ed
pat ted	seat ed	shout ed
card ed	treat ed	pound ed
cart ed	mind ed	halt ed
part ed	slight ed	want ed

Reading lesson.

James has thatched his little cottage.

He has worked hard to-day.

He is very much tired.

He should be kindly treated.

The hen has hatched some very pretty chickens.

We counted more than a dozen.

We are all much pleased with them.

---

* See the rule when *ed* is to be pronounced as a distinct syllable, and when not, Part III. Chapter 18.

Chapter 4.

Promiscuous reading lessons.

Section 1.

Hay making.

Hark! what noise is that? It is the mower whetting his sithe. He is going to cut down the grass, and the pretty flowers. The sithe is very sharp. Do not go too near it.

Come into this field. See, all the grass is cut down. There is a great number of men and women, with their forks and rakes. They toss, and spread, and turn the new-mown grass. Now they are making it into cocks. How hard they work! Come, let us help to make hay.

O it is very hot!

No matter; we must make hay while the sun shines. How sweet the hay smells! When the hay is quite dry, it must be made into stacks.

Hay is for sheep, and cows, and horses, to eat, in winter, when grass does not grow.

Section 2.

Thunder and lightning.

There has not been any rain for a great while. The ground is very dry, and hard. The grass does not look green as it used to do. It is brown: it is scorched by the sun. If it do not rain soon, we must water the trees and flowers, else they will die.

The sun does not shine now : but it is very hot. It is quite sultry. There is no wind at all. The leaves on the trees do not move. The sky looks very black ; and how dark it is! Ha! what a bright light shone through the room! Now it is gone It did not last long. What was it? It was lightning.

Lightning comes from the clouds.

Now it lightens again.

What a noise there is in the air, just over our heads!

That is thunder.

How loud the thunder is !

It begins to rain. O what large drops ! Now it rains very fast.

Section 3.

Harvest.

The storm is over. It is very pleasant now. It is not so hot as it was before the rain came, and the thunder, and the lightning. How sweet the flowers smell! The trees, and the hedges, and the grass, look fresh and green.

Let us go into the corn fields to see if the corn is ripe. Yes, it is quite brown: it is ripe. There are the reapers, with their sharp sickles. They are cutting down the corn.

This is a grain of corn. This is an ear of corn What grows upon a single stalk, is called an ear. The stalk on which the corn grows, makes straw. This bundle of corn is called a sheaf. This is a shock. There are many sheaves in a shock.

When the corn is dry, it must be taken to the barn, to be thrashed. Then it must be sent to the mill, to be ground. When it is ground, it is called flour.

There are some little boys and girls picking up ears of corn. They are gleaning. There is a poor old man gleaning. He is very old, indeed.

His hair is quite white. His hands shake. He is almost too old to work; but he does not like to be idle. He has come a great way to pick up a few ears of corn; he is very much tired with walking about the fields, and stooping. He has dropped one of his little bundles of corn. Take it up and carry it to him. Speak kindly to the poor old man. Now let us pick up a few ears of corn for him. Take them to him. They will help to make a loaf of bread for him.

Section 4.
The Partridge.

Hark! there is a gun let off; and a bird has dropped down, just at our feet. Ah! it is bloody. Its wing is broken. It cannot fly any further. Poor thing! how it flutters! It is going to die. Now it does not stir. It is quite dead.

What bird is it? It is a partridge. There is a man with a gun in his hand. He is coming to fetch the partridge. Now he has let off his gun again. He has shot a very pretty bird indeed. It has red, and green, and purple feathers. What a fine tail it has! This bird is a great deal larger than a partridge. It is a pheasant.

Section 5.

The Orchard.

Let us go into the orchard. The apples are ripe. We must gather them. Fetch that little basket. There is a man in that tree. He will gather all the apples that grow on those high branches. Do not climb up the ladder. Gather the apples that are on the ground.

Look at those poor little girls standing at the gate. They want to come in. They want some apples. Their fathers and mothers have no fields, nor orchards, nor gardens.

Poor little girls! Shall we give them some apples?

Yes; fill that basket with fine, ripe apples, and give them to the little girls. O, now they are glad. How kindly they thank us! They are gone home. Perhaps, they will give some of their apples to their fathers and mothers, and little brothers and sisters.

Section 6.

The Robin.

Scrape your shoes. Do not bring any dirt into the room.

Come in. If your hands are very cold, rub them: if you hold them to the fire, you will have chilblains, which are very painful indeed.

Shut the window, Ann.

Ha! there is a pretty little robin flying about the room. We must give him something to eat. Fetch some bread for him. Throw the crumbs on the floor.

Eat, pretty robin, eat.

He will not eat: I believe, he is afraid of us. He looks about, and wonders where he is!

O, he begins to eat! He is not afraid now. He is very hungry.

How pretty it is to see him pick up the crumbs, and hop about upon the floor, the table, and the chairs! Perhaps, when he has done eating, he will sing us a song.

But we must not keep him here always. Birds

do not like to be shut up in a room, or in a cage. They like to fly about in the air, and to pick up seeds and worms in the fields, and to hop about on the grass, and to sing perched upon the branches of high trees. And in spring, how busy they are building their nests, and taking care of their young ones!

Robin has flown against the window: he wants to get out. Well, we will open the window, and, if he chooses, he may fly away.

There, now he is gone.

When he is hungry, he may come again. We will give him some more crumbs.

Section 7.

The Seasons.

It is winter now, cold winter. It freezes. The pond is frozen, and the river is frozen. We can walk upon the river now. Do not be afraid; the ice is very thick, and hard. There is a man skating; and there are some boys sliding.

It snows. How fast it snows! We cannot see

the grass, nor the gravel walk, nor the road. There is thick snow upon the trees, and the hedges. How pretty the snow is! Snow comes from the clouds.

Bring some snow to the fire. See, how it melts! It is all gone now: there is nothing but water. When the sun shines, and the weather is warmer, the snow that is on the ground will melt; and it will sink into the earth as the rain does.

When winter is quite over, spring will come again. O spring is very pleasant! there will be daisies, and cowslips, and a great many pretty flowers; there will be blossoms and green leaves upon the trees; and there will be young lambs, and chickens, and goslings. The birds will sing sweetly; and they will be very busy picking up bits of hay, and moss, and wool, to build their nests with: and the cuckoo will sing cuckoo, cuckoo. The days will be longer than they are in winter, and the weather will be warmer.

When spring is over, it will be summer. Then the weather is hot, and the days are long. There will be hay time and harvest, and thunder and lightning. The fruit will be ripe; cherries, currants, peaches, and plums, and a great many other kinds of fruit; and there will be moss roses that smell so sweet, and fine pinks.

When summer is over, the days will become short; there will be very few flowers left, in the fields, and in the gardens; the leaves on the trees, will begin to fade, and they will fall off. The weather will be cold, and there will be thick fogs. But it will not be winter as soon as summer is over. No; it will be autumn. Then apples and pears, filberts and walnuts, will be ripe.

When autumn is over, winter, cold winter, will come again; and frost, ice, and snow, and short, dark days, and long nights.

Spring, summer, autumn, winter. And what are these called?

They are called seasons.

Section 8.

The Lamb.

It is very cold. And how high the wind is! There is a tree blown down.

What has that man in his arms?

It is a young lamb.

Poor thing! how it bleats! It wants its mother. It is crying for her. I wish she could hear it: but she cannot hear; she is dead.

Pray, shepherd, take good care of the little lamb, and give it nice new milk to drink, and keep it warm; and when it can take care of itself, and the weather is pleasant, let it sport and frisk about in the fields, and be very merry.

We must not go any further now. The sky looks very black. I think there will be a heavy shower soon.

Section 9.

Sheep shearing.

What is that man doing to the sheep?

He is cutting off their soft, thick wool. He is shearing them. The large scissors that he has in his hand, are called shears. It does not hurt the sheep to have their wool cut off. They can do without it now, the weather is so warm.

And will the wool be thrown away?

No. It will not be thrown away. Charles's coat is made of wool. Blankets are made of wool; and so are carpets, and flannel, and a great many things. But the wool must be carded first, and spun, and woven, and died.

There is a woman spinning. She has a very large wheel. That is wool which she has in her hand. She is spinning for her husband, and her children.

That little girl is carding the wool. She is making it ready for her mother to spin.

Section 10.

Boys looking for Birds' nests.

What are those boys looking for, in the hedges, and among the bushes?

Little boys, what do you want?

We are looking for birds' nests. We want some eggs, and some young birds.

But why should you take the eggs, and the

young birds? They will do you no good; and the old birds who have taken so much pains to build their nests, will be very sorry, indeed, to lose their eggs, and their young ones. You cannot feed the young birds so well as they can; nor take so good care of them; nor keep them warm at nights.

Some little boys who steal young birds from their soft, warm nests, and from the parent birds, soon grow tired of them, and forget to feed them; then the little birds die! The old birds are never tired of their young ones; and never leave off feeding them, till they can fly, and take care of themselves.

A little boy took a young bird from its nest; but very soon he was tired of it, and did not like the trouble of feeding it, and wanted to get rid of it. He asked some little boys whom he met, if they would have it; but they said they did not want it. They told him to carry it back to the nest whence he had taken it; but he would not: he threw the bird into the water, and drowned it. O what a cruel boy!

Little boys, if you find any nests, do not rob the poor birds of their eggs, and their young ones. You may look at the little birds, in their nests: but do not frighten them; do not hurt them; do not take them away from their kind parents, and from their soft, clean, warm nests. You would not like, (would you?) that any body should take you from your fathers and mothers, and your own homes; and keep you always shut up, quite alone, in a very small place; and feed you in a very strange way, or almost starve you to death.

Chapter 5*.

Words of three syllables.

Section 1.

The accent on the first syllable.

All the syllables short †.

Al pha bet	ca ta logue
a va rice	cha rac ter
bash ful ness	cin na mon
blun der er	cot ta ges
ca bi net	co vet ous
can dle stick	dif fer ence
ca nis ter	em pe ror
car pen ter	ex cel lent

* The arrangement of the words in this chapter, besides aiding, in some degree, the pronunciation, will render the learner's progress much easier than those arrangements, which require frequent and perplexing transitions from a word composed of short syllables, to another of long ones, and *vice versa*.

† To prevent embarrassment from too many subdivisions, the middle sounds, in this chapter, are included under the short; and the broad sounds, under the long ones.

WORDS OF

All the syllables short.

Fa ther less	nec ta rine
fish er man	nut crack ers
fri vo lous	o ran ges
gar den er	pil fer er
ga ther ing	pri son er
ge ne rous	pros per ous
gen tle man	pu nish ment
gin ger bread	quar rel some
go vern ess	quick sil ver
go vern or	ra ven ous
grand fa ther	rot ten ness
grand mo ther	se ve ral
grass hop per	se pa rate
hand ker chief	shut tle cock
hus band man	sil ver smith
ka len dar	spec ta cles
jes sa mine	ten der ness
la ven der	tra vel ler
le ve ret	trou ble some
li be ral	va ga bond
mid sum mer	web foot ed
mil li ner	wick ed ness
mi nis ter	won der ful

THREE SYLLABLES.

All the syllables long.

Cru ci fy
de vi ate
ea si ly
la dy fly

po e try
rose ma ry
se cre cy
sla ve ry

The two first short, the last long.

Af ter ward
but ter fly
co lum bine
com pa ny
con tra ry
e ve ry
e ver green
ex er cise
flat te ry
gal le ry
goose ber ry
his to ry
ho nes ty
in dus try
in fan cy
man ful ly

me mo ry
mo de rate
mo dest ly
mul ber ry
nur se ry
pa ra dise
po ver ty
pre sent ly
pro per ly
rasp ber ry
sa tis fy
slip pe ry
some bo dy
vic to ry
wil ling ly
yes ter day

The two first long, the last short.

A pri cot	hay ma ker
beau ti ful	la zi ness
du ti ful	moun te bank
coun te nance	sau ci ness
cu ri ous	shoe ma ker
glo ri ous	vi o let
gree di ness	vi o lent

The first short, the others long.

Ap pe tite	har mo ny
ar ti choke	in di go
ca li co	mer ri ly
ca te chise	ob sti nate
di mi ty	pet ti coat
e ne my	pret ti ly
fur ni ture	sig ni fy

The first long, the others short.

Al ma nac	fool ish ness
cow ard ice	hy a cinth
dan ger ous	i dle ness
di a per	la bour er
di a logue	pow er ful
di a mond	or na ment
e ven ing	qui et ness

THREE SYLLABLES.

The middle short, the others long.

Al rea dy	night in gale
care ful ly	no bo dy
cham ber maid	peace a bly
de cen cy	peace ful ly
faith ful ly	play fel low
gor man dize	pri vate ly
grate ful ly	straw ber ry
i vo ry	ta ble cloth
mourn ful ly	wheel bar row

The middle long, the others short.

Ac ci dent	in do lent
a i mal	ig no rant
ar ro gant	in no cent
brick lay er	in so lent
clean li ness	me di cine
con so nant	mer ci ful
daf fo dil	mer ri ment
di li gence	mis chiev ous
dif fi cult	of fi cer
e le phant	plen ti ful
gun pow der	pro vi dence
hap pi ness	quad ru ped

Reading lesson,

adapted to the preceding section.

White and black mulberries.

A fine large apricot.

Yellow jessamine.

Pink, and blue, and white hyacinths.

How sweet the violets smell!

A silk handkerchief.

A damask or diaper tablecloth.

Muslin, calico, and dimity, are made of cotton.

Cotton grows in a pod, on a small tree, in warm countries.

A quadruped is an animal with four feet.

Cows, and sheep, and horses, are quadrupeds.

An elephant is the largest of quadrupeds.

Ivory is the tusk, or teeth, of elephants.

A leveret is a young hare.

Nobody that is able to work, should be idle.

Learn something useful every day.

Beautiful animals are not the most useful.

THREE SYLLABLES.

Section 2.

The accent on the second syllable.

All the syllables short.

A bun dance	in debt ed
ad van tage	in dul gence
a mend ment	in struct er
a no ther	mis con duct
ap pren tice	neg lect ful
at ten tive	of fen sive
com mand ment	sub mis sive
con si der	um brel la
con tent ment	un plea sant
dis trust ful	when e ver
en dea vour	what e ver

All the syllables long.

de mure ly	po ta to
hu mane ly	se rene ly
po lite ly	se vere ly

The two first short, the last long.

Ad ven ture	dis tinct ly
con tem plate	dis tri bute
con ti nue	ex act ly
dis fi gure	un clean ly

I 3

The two first long, the last short.

Be tray er	de stroy er
cre a tor	de vour er
de ceit ful	di vi ded
de co rum	o bli ging
de light ful	re deem er
de lu sive	re main der
de mure ness	re ward er
de ni al	se du cer

The first short, the others long.

Bal co ny	sin cere ly
com plete ly	un ea sy
im pure ly	un seem ly
in qui ry	un ti dy

The first long, the others short.

Be gin ning	re sem ble
be long ing	e le ven
de can ter	e pis tle
de pend ent	me cha nic
for got ten	re sist ance
re luc tant	re venge ful
re mem ber	to ge ther
re miss ness	wher e ver

THREE SYLLABLES.

The middle long, the others short.

A bu sive	em broi der
ac quaint ance	em ploy ment
a gree ment	en light en
a muse ment	en tice ment
as su rance	for sa ken
con tri vance	in de cent
dis ci ple	in hu man
dis dain ful	un a ble
dis grace ful	un grate ful

Reading lesson.

When you read, or speak, pronounce every word distinctly.

Endeavour to improve, and try to remember what you have learned.

Be kind and obliging to every body.

Let all your amusements be innocent.

Remember a kindness, and never be ungrateful.

A revengeful temper shows a bad heart, and is very troublesome to him that has it.

Section 3.

The accent on the last syllable.

All the syllables short.

Con tra dict	in ter mix
dis con tent	re com mend
in cor rect	un der stand

The two first short, the last long.

Dis a gree	in ter cede
dis ap point	ma ga zine
dis en gage	un der take
en ter tain	vo lun teer

The first short, the others long.

Dis o bey	mis be have
dis o blige	re fu gee
dis u nite	un be lief

The middle short, the others long.

O ver hear	o ver bear
o ver take	su per scribe
o ver flow	su per fine

The middle long, the others short.

Com plai sance	cor re spond
com pre hend	re pre sent
con de scend	re pri mand

Reading lesson,

adapted to the preceding section.

Never disagree with your playfellows.

If you disoblige others, they will disoblige you.

Some children are apt to contradict, but every body dislikes such a temper.

When you do not understand a thing, and modestly inquire, your friends will condescend to instruct you.

To superscribe signifies to write on the top or outside. Charles will superscribe or direct his letter.

To reprimand signifies to reprove a person for some fault. James has received a reprimand for neglecting his lesson.

Never try to overhear persons who are speaking privately.

If any thing disappoints you, try to be content.

People who can read well, and who love to read, can entertain themselves with books.

Chapter 6.

Promiscuous reading lesson.

Section 1.

The Sun.

The sun rises in the east; and when he rises, it is day.

He shines upon the trees and the houses, and upon the water; and every thing looks sparkling and beautiful, when he shines upon it. He gives us light and heat; it is he that makes it warm. He makes the fruit ripen, and the corn ripen. If he did not shine upon the fields, and upon the gardens, nothing would grow.

Sometimes he takes off his crown of bright rays, and wraps up his head in thin silver clouds, and then we may look at him; but when there are no clouds, and he shines with all his brightness at noonday, we cannot look at him, for he would dazzle our eyes, and make us blind. Only the eagle can look at him then: the eagle with his strong piercing eye can gaze upon him always.

When the sun is going to rise in the morning, and make it day, the lark flies up in the sky to meet him, and sings sweetly in the air; and the cock crows loud to tell every body that he is coming: but the owl and the bat fly away when they see him, and hide themselves in old walls and hollow trees; and the lion and the tiger go into their dens and caves, where they sleep all the day.

He shines in all countries, all over the earth. He is the most beautiful and glorious creature that can be seen in the whole world.

Section 2.

The Moon.

The moon shines to give us light in the night, when the sun is set. She is very beautiful, and white like silver. We may look at her always, for she is not so bright as to dazzle our eyes, and she never scorches us. She is mild and gentle. She lets even the little glow-worms shine, which are quite dark by day. The stars shine all round her, but she seems larger and brighter than the stars, and looks like a large pearl amongst a great many small sparkling diamonds.

When you are asleep, she shines through your curtains with her gentle beams, and seems to say, Sleep on, poor little tired boys, I will not disturb you. The nightingale sings to her, and sings better than all the birds of the air. She sits upon a thorn, and sings sweetly all the night long, while the dew lies upon the grass, and every thing around is still and silent.

Section 3.

The Swan.

All birds that swim in the water are webfooted. Their toes are joined together by a skin that grows between them; that is being webfooted; and it helps the birds to swim well, for then their feet are like the fins of a fish.

The swan is a large bird, larger than a goose.

Its bill is red, but the sides of it are black; and it has black about its eyes. Its legs are dusky, but its feet are red, and it is webfooted. Its body is all white, as white as snow, and very beautiful. It has a very long neck. It lives in rivers and lakes; and eats plants that grow in the water, and seeds, and little insects, and snails.

It does not look pretty when it walks upon the ground, for it cannot walk well; but when it is in the water swimming smoothly along, arching its long neck, and dipping its white breast, with which it makes way through the water, it is the most graceful of all birds.

The swan builds her nest amongst the reeds and rushes. The nest is made of sticks and long grass; and it is very large and high. The eggs which she lays, are white, and very large, larger a great deal than a goose's egg; and she sits upon them for two months: then they are hatched, and the young ones come out. They are called cygnets. They are not white at first, but grayish.

If any body were to come near the swan, when she is in the nest, sitting upon her eggs, or when she has young ones, she would fly at him; for she is very fierce to defend her young: and if he were to come to take them away, she would beat him down with her strong wings, and perhaps break his arm. The swan lives a very great while.

Section 4.

The Hare.

Ha! what is there amongst the furze? I can see only its eyes. It has very large full eyes. It is a hare. It is in its form, or house, squatting down amongst the bushes to hide itself, for it is very fearful.

The hare is very innocent and gentle. Its colour is brown; but in countries which are very cold, it turns white as snow. It has a short bushy tail; its lip is parted, and very hairy; and it always moves its lips. Its hind legs are very long, that it may run the better. The hare feeds upon herbs, and roots, and the bark of young trees, and green corn; and sometimes it will creep through the hedge, and steal into the gardens, to eat pinks and a little parsley; and it loves to play and skip about by moonlight, and to bite the tender blades of grass, when the dew is upon them; but in the daytime it sleeps in its form.

She sleeps with her eyes open, because she is very fearful and timid; and when she hears the least noise, she starts, and pricks up her large ears. And when the huntsman sounds his horn, and the poor harmless hare hears the dogs coming, she runs away very swiftly straight forward, stretching her legs, and leaves them all behind. But the dogs pursue her, and she grows tired, and cannot run so fast as at first. Then she doubles, and turns, and runs back to her form, that the hounds may not find her; but they run with their noses to the ground, smelling till they have found her out. So when she has run five or six miles, at last she stops, and pants for breath, and can run no further. Then the hounds come up, and tear her, and kill her.

When she is dead, her little limbs which moved so fast, grow quite stiff, and cannot move at all. Her poor little heart, that beat so quick, is quite stiff and cold; and her round full eyes are dull and dim; and her soft furry skin is all torn and bloody.

Section 5.

The good Boy.

The good boy loves his parents very dearly. He always minds what they say to him, and tries to please them. If they desire him not to do a thing, he does it not: if they desire him to do a thing, he does it. When they deny him what he wants, he does not grumble, or pout out his lips, or look angry: but he thinks that his parents know what is proper for him, better than he does, because they are wiser than he is.

He loves his teachers, and all who tell him what is good. He likes to read, and to write, and to learn something fresh every day. He hopes that if he lives to be a man, he shall know a great many things, and be very wise and good.

He is kind to his brothers, and sisters, and all his little playfellows. He never fights, nor quarrels with them, nor calls them names. When he sees them do wrong, he is sorry, and tries to persuade them to do better.

He does not speak rudely to any body. If he sees any persons who are lame, or crooked, or very old, he does not laugh at them, nor mock them; but he is glad when he can do them any service.

He is kind even to dumb creatures: for he knows that though they cannot speak, they can feel as well as we. Even those animals which he does not think pretty, he takes care not to hurt. He likes very much to see the birds pick up bits of hay, and moss, and wool, to build their nests with; and he likes to see the hen sitting on her nest, or feeding her young ones; and to see the little birds in their nest, and hear them chirp. Sometimes, he looks about in the bushes, and in the trees, and amongst the strawberry plants, to find nests: but when he has found them, he only just peeps at them; he would rather not see the little birds, than frighten them, or do them any harm.

He never takes any thing that does not belong to him, or meddles with it, without leave. When he walks in his father's garden, he does not pull flowers, or gather fruit, unless he is told that he may do so. The apples that are fallen on the ground, he picks up, and carries to his mother.

He never tells a lie. If he has done any mischief, he confesses it, and says he is very sorry, and will try to do so no more: and nobody can be angry with him.

When he lies down at night, he tries to remember all he has been doing, and learning in the day. If he has done wrong, he is sorry, and hopes he shall do so no more; and that God who is so good, will love and bless him.—He loves to pray to God, and to hear and read about him; and to go with his parents and friends to worship God.

Every body that knows this good boy, loves him, and speaks well of him, and is kind to him: and he is very happy.

Part III.

Words less familiar to children—Correspondent reading lessons—Miscellaneous articles—Rules for spelling, and pronunciation.

When the learner has been carefully taught the lessons, contained in the first and second parts of the book, and been confirmed in the general principles of pronunciation, it will be less necessary (even if it were practicable) to pursue the preceding mode of arrangement, to enable him to pronounce the words in the remaining part of the work. Some aid he will occasionally receive: but, in general he will now derive more advantage from the exercise of his memory and judgment. The words of the first chapter are, however, such as children frequently hear; and the arrangement is calculated to prevent discordant and difficult transitions.

In arranging the words into syllables, the author has not considered the letters, or terminations, tion, tious, scious, science, &c. as distinct syllables. By dividing these terminations, the gradations in spelling a word that contains them, are easy to the learner; and the perplexity of many different and irregular combinations, is avoided.—See the nineteenth chapter, on the division of syllables.

Chapter 1.

Words of three and more syllables.

Section 1.

Words ending in *tion*, &c. pronounced as two syllables, with the accent on the first syllable.

1. The accented syllable short*.

Ac ti on	mar ti al
cap ti ous	men ti on
con sci ence	mil li on
con sci ous	mi ni on
fac ti ous	mis si on
fac ti on	nup ti al
frac ti on	op ti on
junc ti on	par ti al
lus ci ous	pas si on
man si on	pen si on

---

* By arranging the words according to the quantity of the accented syllable, pronunciation is aided; the transition from word to word is easy; and the inconvenience of the double accent, is avoided.

Tion, &c. in this section, are pronounced thus,

Tion and sion................ like *shun*.

TRISYLLABLES.

pil li on
pi ni on
pre ci ous
sec ti on
ses si on

spe ci al
suc ti on
unc ti on
ver si on
vi ci ous

2. The accented syllable long.

an ci ent
auc ti on
bra si er
cau ti on
cau ti ous
gla zi er
gra ci ous
ho si er
mo ti on
na ti on

no ti on
pa ti ence
pa ti ent
por ti on
po ti on
quo ti ent
so ci al
spa ci ous
spe ci ous
sta ti on

Tious, scious, and cious .... like *shus*.
Science and tience .... like *shence*.
Tial and cial .... like *shal*.
Zier and sier .... like *zhur*.
Ion, preceded by *l* or *n* .... like *yun*.

TRISYLLABLES.

Section 2.

Words of three syllables.

Accent on the first syllable.

1. The accented syllable short.

ac cu rate	jus ti fy
af fa ble	lux u ry
be ne fit	mas cu line
cha ri ty	no vel ty
com pa ny	ob sta cle
cus tom er	per se cute
e vi dent	pos si ble
her mit age	spec ta cle
im pu dent	tes ta ment

2. The accented syllable long.

a li en	ho li ness
co gen cy	kna vish ly
di a dem	l na tic
dra pe ry	mu ta ble
du ra ble	no ti fy
fe ver ish	pi e ty
fu ne ral	re cent ly
glo ri fy	va can cy
grace ful ness	vi o late

TRISYLLABLES.

Accent on the second syllable.

1. The accented syllable short.

ac com plish
af fect ing
at tend ance
con nect ed
con sump tive
de li ver
de mon strate
dis co ver
dis ho nest
do mes tic

em bel lish
for get ful
im mo dest
in ha bit
in ter pret
oc cur rence
of fend er
to bac co
tri umph ant
un com mon

2. The accented syllable long.

ad vi ser
ap pear ance
at tain ment
ca the dral
de ceiv er
de ci sive
de lu sive
dif fu sive
en vi rons
ex al ted

he ro ic
ma ture ly
per fu mer
per sua sive
po ma tum
re view er
se cure ly
spec ta tor
tri bu nal
un time ly

Section 3.

Words ending in *tion*, &c. pronounced as three syllables, with the accent on the second syllable.

1. The accented syllable short.

Af fec ti on	es sen ti al
at ten ti on	ex pres si on
com pa ni on	in struc ti on
com pas si on	li cen ti ous
con di ti on	ob jec ti on
con fes si on	per fec ti on
de li ci ous	pro vin ci al
de scrip ti on	sub stan ti al
e lec ti on	suf fi ci ent

2. The accented syllable long.

ca pa ci ous	o ra ti on
con clu si on	pol lu ti on
con fu si on	pro por ti on
cre a ti on	re la ti on
de vo ti on	sal va ti on
fal la ci ous	temp ta ti on
foun da ti on	trans la ti on
im pa ti ent	va ca ti on
nar ra ti on	vex a ti on

POLYSYLLABLES.

Section 4.

Words of four syllables.

Accent on the first syllable.

1. The accented syllable short.

ad mi ra ble	in te rest ing
an nu al ly	mi se ra ble
ca ter pil lar	ne ces sa ry
cha ri ta ble	ob sti na cy
com fort a ble	pro fit a ble
di li gent ly	se cre ta ry
ha ber dash er	to le ra ble
ho nour a ble	tran si to ry
in ti ma cy	ve ge ta ble

2. The accented syllable long.

a mi a ble	mo ment a ry
a vi a ry	mu si cal ly
beau ti ful ly	nu me rous ly
co pi ous ly	or di na ry
dan ger ous ly	pu ri fi er
for mi da ble	rea son a ble
fraud u lent ly	right e ous ness
hu mour ous ly	sea son a bly
lu mi na ry	va ri a ble

I.

POLYSYLLABLES.

Accent on the second syllable.

1. The accented syllable short.

ab surd i ty	in dus tri ous
ad ver si ty	in ha bi tant
bar ba ri ty	no bi li ty
be ne vo lent	par ti cu lar
ca pa ci ty	pros pe ri ty
com mend a ble	ri di cu lous
con si der ate	sin ce ri ty
di mi nu tive	so li cit ous
ex pe ri ment	ty ran ni cal
ex tra va gant	un man ner ly

2. The accented syllable long.

ab ste mi ous	ex ceed ing ly
a bu sive ly	ex cu sa ble
a gree a ble	gram ma ri an
cen so ri ous	in ca pa ble
con ve ni ent	in de cen cy
de plo ra ble	la bo ri ous
de si ra ble	ma te ri al
e lu ci date	ob scu ri ty
e nu me rate	su pe ri or
er ro ne ous	va ri e ty

POLYSYLLABLES.

Accent on the third syllable.

1. The accented syllable short.

ac ci dent al	in con sist ent
ap pre hen sive	in of fen sive
be ne fac tor	ma le fac tor
com pli ment al	ma nu fac ture
com pre hen sive	me mo ran dum
cor re spond ence	or na ment al
dis ad van tage	pa ra ly tic
dis con tent ed	sci en ti fic
e pi de mic	un be com ing
in ad vert ence	u ni ver sal

2. The accented syllable long.

af fi da vit	eu ro pe an
an no ta tor	hy me ne al
an te ce dent	ig no ra mus
bar ri ca do	in co he rent
bas ti na do	in ter fe rence
com ment a tor	me di a tor
dan de li on	mo de ra tor
dis a gree ment	op por tune ly
dis ap point ed	se mi co lon
dis com po sure	vir tu o so

Section 5.

Words ending in *tion*, &c. pronounced as four syllables, with the accent on the third syllable.

1. The accented syllable short.

a va ri ci ous	in au spi ci ous
con de scen si on	in suf fi ci ent
con sci en ti ous	op po si ti on
de fi ni ti on	pe ni ten ti al
dis qui si ti on	pre ju di ci al
e qui noc ti al	pre pos ses si on
ex pe di ti on	re qui si ti on
ex pe di ti ous	sa tis fac ti on
im per fec ti on	su per sti ti ous

2. The accented syllable long.

ab so lu ti on	ef fi ca ci ous
ad mi ra ti on	e mu la ti on
ap pli ca ti on	in cli na ti on
ap pro ba ti on	in vi ta ti on
com pi la ti on	ob ser va ti on
con ver sa ti on	pre pa ra ti on
cul ti va ti on	pro vo ca ti on
de mon stra ti on	re sig na ti on
e du ca ti on	re so lu ti on

Section 6.

Words of five syllables.

Accent on the second syllable.

1. The accented syllable short.

a bo mi na ble	in com pa ra ble
a po the ca ry	in es ti ma ble
con si der a ble	pre pa ra to ry
con ti nu al ly	re po si to ry
dis ho nour a ble	un cha ri ta ble
dis in te rest ed	un com fort a ble
ex pla na to ry	un go vern a ble
i ma gin a ry	un ne ces sa ry
im prac ti ca ble	un par don a ble

2. The accented syllable long.

cen so ri ous ly	ma te ri al ly
com mu ni ca ble	mys te ri ous ly
com mu ni ca tive	no to ri ous ly
fe lo ni ous ly	ob se qui ous ness
im me di ate ly	pe cu ni a ry
in du bi ta ble	re me di a ble
in vi o la ble	re mu ne ra tive
la bo ri ous ly	un rea son a ble
lux u ri ant ly	vic to ri ous ly

POLYSYLLABLES.

Accent on the third syllable.
1. The accented syllable short.

a ca de mi cal
al pha bet i cal
a ni mo si ty
an ni ver sa ry
chris ti an i ty
con tra dic to ry
cu ri o si ty
ge o gra phi cal
hos pi tal i ty
im mo ral i ty

in ci vil i ty
in dis pen sa ble
in fi del i ty
in sig ni fi cant
ir re sist i ble
li be ral i ty
ma nu fac to ry
sa tis fac to ry
sen si bi li ty
u ni ver si ty

2. The accented syllable long.

am bi gu i ty
ce re mo ni ous
con tu me li ous
dis a gree a ble
dis o be di ence
ex com mu ni cate
im ma te ri al
im me mo ri al
im pro pri e ty
in con so la ble

in con ve ni ent
in de cli na ble
in ex cu sa ble
in ge nu i ty
in ter me di ate
jus ti fi a ble
me ri to ri ous
mis cel la ne ous
op por tu ni ty
un ac count a ble

Accent on the fourth syllable.

cha rac ter is tic
ec cle si as tic
en thu si as tic
e pi gram ma tic

ex pe ri ment al
su per a bun dance
ad mi nis tra tor
mul ti pli ca tor

Accent on the first syllable.

cus tom a ri ly
de di ca to ry
fi gu ra tive ly
la bo ra to ry

ne ces sa ri ly
or di na ri ly
po ly syl la ble
vo lun ta ri ly

Section 7.

Words ending in *tion*, &c. pronounced as five syllables, with the accent on the fourth syllable.

ab bre vi a ti on
ac com mo da ti on
al le vi a ti on
cir cum lo cu ti on
com mu ni ca ti on
con si der a ti on
con ti nu a ti on
de li ber a ti on
de ter mi na ti on

e qui vo ca ti on
ex a mi na ti on
in ter pre ta ti on
in ter ro ga ti on
jus ti fi ca ti on
re com mend a ti on
sig ni fi ca ti on
sub or di na ti on
ver si fi ca ti on

Section 8.

Words of six and seven syllables, properly accented.

in vó lun ta ri ly
un reá son a ble ness
ce re mó ni ous ly
dis o bé di ent ly
em blem á ti cal ly
in con sí der ate ly
in con vé ni ent ly
in ter ró ga to ry
me ri tó ri ous ly
re com ménd a to ry
su per án nu a ted
su per nú me ra ry

dis sa tis fác to ry
e ty mo ló gi cal
fa mi li ár i ty
im mu ta bí li ty
in fal li bí li ty
pe cu li ár i ty
pre des ti ná ri an
su per in ténd en cy
u ni ver sál i ty
im ma te ri ál i ty
in cor rup ti bí li ty
va le tu di ná ri an

Section 9.

Reading lesson,

adapted to the sections of this chapter.

A kind action gives pleasure, both to ourselves and the person to whom we are kind.

Violent passions make people miserable.

Charles was very ill, but he was patient. His

friends treated him with great attention and compassion.

If we would gain knowledge, we must study very diligently.

A good education is a great blessing.

A caterpillar changes into a butterfly. All the butterflies, which we see flying about, were caterpillars once.

An apothecary sells medicines.

The haberdasher sells tape and thread, and pins and needles, and other small wares.

To think too highly of ourselves, is unbecoming and ridiculous.

If we expect others to love us, without our being kind and good, we shall be disappointed.

To fret because others are happier than we are, is very unreasonable.

We should remember, that if we let an opportunity of doing good, pass away, it will never return.

To do a thing voluntarily, signifies to do it willingly.

To be superannuated, is, to be unable to do things, on account of old age.

A valetudinarian is one that is sickly.

Chapter 2.

Promiscuous reading lessons.

Section 1.

The Boy and the Looking-glass.

A little boy, when his father and mother were from home, was playing at ball in a room where there was a looking-glass.

Before he began to play, he had turned the back of the looking-glass towards him, for fear he should break the glass. It would have been better, if he had gone out of doors to play at ball. As he was not a careless boy, I wonder he was not afraid of breaking the windows, as well as the looking-glass; but I suppose he did not think of that.

Whilst he was playing, and, perhaps, not thinking at all about the looking-glass, his ball struck the wooden back, and broke the glass. When he saw the mischief he had done, he was very sorry; and, I believe, he was afraid his father and mother would be displeased with him.

When his parents came home, he went to his father, and said; "Father, I have broken the best looking-glass in the house! and I am very sorry for it." His father looked kindly at him, and said, "I would rather that all the looking-glasses in my house, should be broken, than that one of my children should tell an untruth."

The little boy hearing his father say this, and seeing that he was not angry, felt comforted; though, I suppose, he wished very much that he had not broken the looking-glass. After that time, when he met with an accident, he confessed it; and would not, on any account, tell an untruth.

Section 2.

The good Boy whose parents are rich.

The good boy whose parents are rich, has fine clothes to wear; and he rides on a pretty little horse, and in a coach; and has servants to wait on him: but he does not, for all that, think that he is better than other boys whose parents are not rich. He knows that all rich people are not good; and that God gives a great deal of money to some persons, in order that they may assist those who are poor.

He speaks very kindly to all his father's servants. He does not call them to wait upon him, when they are at their meals, or very busy. If he wants them to do him a service, he asks them prettily; and thanks them for what they do for him. He never gives them any trouble that he can avoid; therefore, he is careful not to make dirt in the house, and not to break any thing, or put it out of its place, and not to tear his clothes. When any of the servants who wait upon him, are ill, he likes to go and see them; and he often thinks of them, and asks how they do.

He likes to go with his father, or his mother, to see poor people, in their cottages; and he gives them almost all the money he has.

When he sees little boys and girls, that are ragged, dirty, and rude, and that have nobody to teach them to read, and to give them good books, he is very sorry for them, and he often says, "If I were a man, and had a great deal of money, I think no person that lived near me should be very poor. I would build a great many pretty cottages for poor people to live in; and every cottage should have belonging to it a garden, and a field, in order that the poor people might have plenty of vegetables, and a cow, and a pig, and some poultry; and they should not pay me much rent. I would give clothes to the little boys and girls; and they should all learn to read, and to write, and to work, and to be very good."

Section 3.

The good Boy whose parents are poor.

The good boy whose parents are poor, rises very early in the morning; and all day long, does as much as he can to help his father and mother.

When he goes to school, he walks quickly, and does not lose time on the road. "My parents," says he, "are very good, to save some of their money, in order that I may learn to read and write; but they cannot give much, nor can they spare me long; therefore I must learn as fast as I can: if any body has time to lose, I am sure I have not. I should be very sorry, when I am a man, not to know how to read very well, in the Bible, and other good books; and when I leave my parents, not to be able to read their letters, and to write them word where I am, and how I do. And I must learn accounts, for when I grow up, I shall have many things to reckon about my work, and what I buy: I shall perhaps have bills to make out, as my father has; and perhaps I shall be employed in a shop."

When he has finished his lessons, he does not stay to play, but runs home; he wants to see his father and mother, and to help them, and to nurse the little baby. He often sees naughty boys in the streets, and in the fields, fight, and steal, and do many sad things; and he hears them swear, and call names, and tell lies: but he does not like to be with them, for fear they should make him as bad as they are; and that any body who sees him with them, should think that he, too, is naughty.

When he is at home, he is very industrious. He takes care of the little children; mends his clothes; knits his stockings; and spins worsted: or he weeds his father's garden, and hoes, and rakes it, and sows seeds in it. Sometimes he goes with his father to work: then he is very glad; and though he is but a little fellow, he works very hard, almost like a man. When he comes home to dinner, he says, " How hungry I am! and how good this bread is, and this bacon! Indeed, I think every thing we have, is very good. I am glad I can work: I hope that I shall soon be able to earn all my clothes, and my food too."

When he sees little boys and girls riding on pretty horses, or in coaches, or walking with ladies and gentlemen, and having on very fine clothes, he does not envy them, nor wish to be like them. He says, " I have often been told, and I have read, that it is God who makes some to be poor, and some rich; that the rich have many troubles which we know nothing of; and that the poor, if they are but good, may be very happy: indeed, I think that when I am good, nobody can be happier than I am."

Section 4.

The attentive and industrious little Girl.

She always minds what her father and mother say to her; and takes pains to learn whatever they are so kind as to teach her. She is never noisy or troublesome: so they like to have her with them, and they like to talk to her, and to instruct her.

She has learned to read so well, and she is so good a girl, that her father has given her several little books, which she reads in, by herself, whenever she likes; and she understands all that is in them.

She knows the meaning of a great many difficult words; and the names of a great many countries, cities, and towns, and she can find them upon a map. She can spell almost every little sentence that her father asks her to spell; and she can write very prettily, even without a copy; and she can do a great many sums on a slate.

Whatever she does, she takes pains to do it well; and when she is doing one thing, she tries not to think of another.

If she has made a mistake, or done any thing wrong, she is sorry for it: and when she is told of a fault, she endeavours to avoid it, another time.

When she wants to know any thing, she asks her father, or her mother, to tell her; and she tries to understand, and to remember what they tell her: but if they do not think proper to answer her questions, she does not teaze them, but says, " When I am older, they will perhaps instruct me;" and she thinks about something else.

She likes to sit by her mother, and sew, or knit. When she sews, she does not take long stitches, or pucker her work; but does it very neatly, just as her mother tells her to do. And she always keeps her work very clean: for if her hands are dirty, she washes them before she begins her work; and when she has finished it, she folds it up, and puts it by, very carefully, in her work-bag, or in a drawer. It is but very seldom indeed that she loses her thread, or needles, or any thing she has to work with. She keeps her needles and thread in her housewife: and she has a pincushion on which she puts her pins. She does not stick needles on her sleeve, or put pins in her mouth: for she has been told those are silly, dangerous tricks; and she always pays attention to what is said to her.

She takes care of her own clothes; and folds them up very neatly. She knows exactly where she puts them; and, I believe, she could find them even in the dark. When she sees a hole in her stockings, or her frock, or any of her clothes, she mends it, or asks her mother to have it mended: she does not wait till the hole is very large; for she remembers what her mother has told her, that "A stitch in time saves nine."

She does not like to waste any thing. She never throws away, or burns, crumbs of bread, or peelings of fruit, or little bits of muslin, or linen, or ends of thread: for she has seen the chickens and the little birds, picking up crumbs, and the pigs feeding upon peelings of fruit; and she has seen the ragman go about gathering rags, which her mother has told her, he sells to people who make paper of them.

When she goes with her mother, into the kitchen, and the dairy, she takes notice of every thing she sees; but she does not meddle with any thing, without leave. She knows how puddings, tarts, butter, and bread, are made.

She can iron her own clothes; and she can make her own bed. She likes to feed the chickens and the young turkeys, and to give them clean water to drink, and to wash themselves in; she likes to work in her little garden, to weed it, and to sow seeds and plant roots in it; and she likes to do little jobs for her mother: she likes to be employed, and she likes to be useful.

If all little girls would be so attentive, and industrious, how they would delight their parents, and their kind friends! and they would be much happier themselves, than when they are obstinate, or idle, or ill-humoured, and will not learn any thing properly, or mind what is said to them.

Chapter 3.

Names of persons and places.

Section 1.

Names of persons.

Accent on the first syllable.

Aa ron	Gil bert	Ma ry
A bel	Han nah	Mat thew
A dam	He len	Mo ses
Ag nes	Hen ry	Na than
An drew	Ho mer	Pe ter
An na	Ho race	Phe be
Ar thur	Hum phrey	Phi lip
Ca leb	I saac	Phil lis
Cæ sar	Ja cob	Ra chel
Cy rus	Jas per	Rich ard
Da vid	Jo seph	Ro bert
Ed ward	Ju dith	Ro ger
Em ma	Lau rence	Sa rah
E phraim	Leo nard	Si mon
Est her	Lew is	Ste phen
Fran ces	Lu cy	Tho mas
Fran cis	Mar tha	Wal ter

Accent on the first syllable

A bi gail
A bra ham
An tho ny
Ar chi bald
Bar ba ra
Ben ja min
Ca ro line
Ca tha rine
Chris to pher
Da ni el
De bo rah
Do ro thy
Fre de ric
Ga bri el
I sa bel

Jef fe ry
Jo na than
Jo shu a
Ly di a
Mar ga ret
Mi cha el
Mor de cai
Ni cho las
O li ver
Sa mu el
Si me on
So lo mon
Ti mo thy
Va len tine
Wil li am

Accent on the second syllable.

A me li a
Bar tho lo mew
Cor ne li us
E li za beth

E ze ki el
Na tha ni el
Pe ne lo pe
The o phi lus

Section 2.

Names of Places.

Countries.

EÚ ROPE	A' SI A
Nór way	Túr key
Swé den	Tár ta ry
Dén márk	Chí na
Rús si a	Ja pán
Gér ma ny	East-I'n dies
Prús si a	Pér si a
Aú stri a	A rá bi a
Bo hé mi a	A' FRI CA
Hún ga ry	Mo róc co
Ba tá vi a	Al giérs
Swít zer land	Tú nis
I' ta ly	Trí po li
France	E' gypt
Spain	Zaá ra
Pór tu gal	Né gro land
E'n gland	Nú bi a
Wales	A bys sí ni a
Scót land	A MÉ RI CA
Iré land	West-I'n dies

PROPER NAMES.

Fló ri da
Geór gi a
Ca ro lí na
Vir gí ni a
Má ry land
Penn syl vá ni a
New-Jér sey
New-York
Rhode-Island
Ver mónt
Con néc ti cut
New-Hámp shire
Mas sa chú setts
Ken túc ky
Ten nes seé

Cá na da
New-Brúns wick
Nó va-Scó ti a
Néw found land
Méx i co
Ca li fór ni a
Lou i si á na
Tér ra-Fír ma
Pe rú
A ma zó ni a
Gui á na
Bra zíl
Pa ra guáy
Chí li
Pa ta gó ni a

Cities.

Lón don
York
Brís tol
Glás gow
E' din burgh
Cork
Dúb lin

Pé ters burg
Mós cow
Stóck holm
Co pen há gen
Bér lin
Wár saw
Dánt zic

Hám burg
A'm ster dam
Rót ter dam
Léy den
Há no ver
Vi én na
Prague
Trent
Fránk fort
Brús sels
Bré da
Bá sil
Bern
Ge né va
Rome
Ná ples
Vé nice
Mán tu a
Leg hórn
Tu rín
Fló rence
Pá ris

Ly' ons
Ma dríd
Bar ce ló na
Cá diz
Lís bon
Bel gráde
Con stan ti nó ple
A lép po
Je rú sa lem
A lex án dri a
Caí ro
Méc ca
Me dí na
Cán ton
Pé kin
Que béc
Há li fax
Bós ton
Phi la dél phi a
Wásh ing ton
Charles-Town
Quí to

Section 3.

Reading lesson,
adapted to the sections of this chapter.

Caroline and Amelia have had a fine morning walk. They met their brothers, Frederic and William; and they all returned cheerful and happy.

Many things that are used in this country, come from other places.—Figs and raisins, oranges and lemons, come from Spain, Italy, and Portugal.

Rice and sugar come from the East and West-Indies. Nutmegs, cinnamon, cloves, pepper, and other spices, come from the East-Indies.

Tobacco grows in Virginia; indigo in Carolina. Tea grows in China; coffee in Turkey and the West-Indies. Prunes and olives grow in France and Spain.

Gold and silver come from Mexico and Peru; marble, from Italy and Turkey; and ivory, from Africa.

Diamonds, pearls, and other precious stones, are found in the East-Indies, and in South America.

Chapter 4.

Promiscuous reading lessons.

Section 1.

The Boy of Dundee.

A poor widow* used to spin and work very hard, in order that she might maintain herself, and her little son. She could not read; but she wished her son might learn, and she sent him to school. As he took pains, he learned to read very well.

When he was about twelve years of age, his mother had a paralytic stroke, and lost the use of her limbs; so she was obliged to lie in bed all day long, and she could not spin, or work any more.

As she had not been able to save any money, she could not hire any body to clean her house, and to work for her; and she was very much distressed. A poor woman, who was her neighbour,

---

* At Dundee, in Scotland.

used sometimes to call in to assist her, and to do little jobs for her: but her son was her great comfort. He said within himself; "I will not let my mother die for want. I will work for her: I will maintain her. God, I hope, will bless me, and prosper my work."

He went to a manufactory that was in the town where he lived; and got some work. Every day, he went to the manufactory, and worked hard, harder than if he had worked for himself alone; and in the evening he brought his wages to his poor mother. Before he went in the morning, he always cleaned the room for his mother; and got their breakfast ready; and did all he could to make her comfortable whilst he was absent.

This good boy thought if his mother could read, she could amuse and employ herself, when he was not with her: so he took a great deal of pains, and taught her to read. And when she had learned, she was highly delighted: "Now," said she, "I am very happy. I am, indeed, confined to my bed, and I cannot work: but I can read the Bible, and that is a great comfort to me; and I have one of the best and kindest of sons."

Section 2.

The little Gardener's gift.

A little boy had a garden; and he had a spade, a rake, and a hoe. He was very fond of working in his garden. One summer, he had in it a great many pretty flowers, a lilach tree, a gooseberry bush, and some peas.

When his peas were large enough to be picked, and his gooseberries were quite ripe, he said to his sister; " I will fetch a basket, and pick all my peas, and my gooseberries, and carry them to the poor lame man on the common: he is so ill now, that he cannot ride on the ass, as he used to do, and go to work."

So the little boy fetched his basket, and was very busy picking his peas and gooseberries: and when he had picked them, he carried them immediately to the poor old man, and put them on the table, and laid some money on the table; all the money he had.

The poor old man was sitting by the fireside, quite alone; for his wife was gone out to work, and his children were a great way off. When he saw the little boy come in, and saw him put the peas, and gooseberries, and money upon the table, he smiled, and looked glad, and thanked him very kindly.

The little boy seemed very happy. His sister was pleased to see him so good to the poor old man, and loved him dearly. I dare say when the old man eat his peas, and his gooseberries, and looked at his money, he thought of the little boy, and said, "I hope God will bless that young gentleman, who is so very good to me."

Section 3.

The little Prisoners.

What pains the little birds take to build their pretty, soft, warm nests! How patiently the hen sits upon her eggs, till they are hatched! How diligently and affectionately both the parents feed, and tend their young ones.

A little boy having found a nest of young sparrows, about a mile from the house where he lived, took it, and returned home. As he went along, with the nest in his hand, he was surprised to see that both the parents of the young birds followed him, at a little distance, and seemed to watch whither he was going.

He thought that they would feed the little birds, if they could get to them: so when he reached home, he put the nest and the young birds in a wire cage, and placed the cage on the outside of a window.

The little birds were hungry, and cried for food. Very soon, both the parents, having small caterpillars in their bills, came to the cage, and gave one to each of the young birds, and seemed glad to see them: then, away they flew for more food.

The old birds continued to feed their young ones very diligently, till they were fledged, and seemed able to fly. Then the little boy took the strongest of the young birds, and put him upon the outside of the cage. When the old birds came, as they always used to do, with worms in their bills, they fluttered about, and seemed very glad that one of their little ones had got out of prison.

They wanted him to fly away; but he had never tried to fly, and he was afraid. Then they flew backwards and forwards from the cage to the top of a chimney that was near, as if to show him how easy it was to fly, and that the journey was but short. At length, away he flew; and he arrived safe at the top of the chimney. Then the old birds fluttered about, as they did when they first saw him on the outside of the cage, and seemed to rejoice very much.

Next day, the boy put another of the birds on the outside of the cage. The old birds were as glad to see him, as they had been to see the other little bird; and took as much pains to persuade him to fly. Then the boy put out the other two birds, which were all he had. When all the little birds were flown, neither they, nor their parents, ever came back to the cage.

I think the little boy must have been much more pleased when he set the young birds free, than he would have been, had he always kept them in prison.

Chapter 5.

Duties of children.

Section 1.

Love your father and mother. They love you very dearly; and they have taken care of you ever since you were born. They loved you, and took care of you, even when you were poor little helpless babies, that could not talk, nor walk about, nor do scarcely any thing but cry, and give a great deal of trouble.

Who is so kind to you as your parents are? Who takes so much pains to instruct you? Who taught you almost every thing you know? Who provides food for you, and clothes, and warm beds to sleep on at nights? Who is so glad when you are pleased, and so sorry when you are troubled? When you are sick, and in pain, who pities you, and tenderly waits upon you, and nurses you? Who prays to God to give you health, and strength, and every good thing?

Obey your parents. They know better what

is proper for you, than you do; and they wish you to be good, and wise, and happy.

If your parents are sick, or in trouble, do all you can to comfort them. If they are poor, work very hard, that you may be able to assist them. Remember how much they have done, and suffered for you.

Section 2.

Love your brothers and sisters. Do not tease nor vex them, nor call them names; and never let your little hands be raised to strike them. If they have any thing which you would like to have, do not be angry with them, or want to get it from them. If you have any thing they like, share it with them.

Your parents grieve when they see you quarrel; they love you all with dear love; and they wish you to love one another, and to live in peace and harmony.

People will not speak, or think, well of you, if you do not behave kindly to your parents, and to your brothers and sisters. "Whom," say they, "will persons love, or be kind to, if they do not love their own father and mother who have done so much for them; and their own brothers and sisters who have the same parents, and the same home as they have, and who are brought up with them?"

Section 3.

Do not meddle with what does not belong to you; nor ever take other people's things, without leave.

Children, never allow yourselves to pluck a flower, or any fruit, that grows in your parents' or other people's gardens, unless you are told that you may do so; never, without leave, take a pin, or a needle, or a bit of thread, from your companions: never, even if your parents are very poor, and have nothing to make a fire with, steal wood from your neighbours' hedges, or branches from their trees. If you steal little things, you will soon learn to steal great things.

Whenever you are tempted to steal, do not say, as some silly, naughty people do: "These are but very little things, nobody will miss them: nobody sees me; and I dare say I shall never be found out." But say: "No, I will not steal: though no man sees me, yet God sees me; and if once I begin, I shall go on stealing. Then every body that knows me, will find me out; and I shall be punished, and despised, and called a thief; and people will be afraid to trust me with any thing that belongs to them. All this, I am sure, will make me very miserable: and oh, what is still worse, God will be displeased with me; for one of his great commandments is, " Thou shalt not steal."

Section 4.

Never tell an untruth.—When you are relating any thing that you have seen, or heard, endeavour to tell it exactly as it was. Do not alter, or invent, any part, to make, as you may think, a prettier story: if you have forgotten any part, say that you have forgotten it. Persons who love the truth, never tell a lie, even in jest.

Consider well before you make a promise. If you say you will do a thing, and you do it not, you will tell a lie: and who then will trust, or believe you? No persons are trusted, or believed, but those who keep their promises, and who speak the truth.

When you have done a wrong, or careless action, do not deny it, even if you are afraid you will be punished for it. If you are sorry for what you have done, and endeavour to do so no more, people will very seldom be angry with you, or punish you. They will love you for speaking the truth; they will think that they may always believe what you say, since they find you will not tell a lie, even to hide a fault, and to prevent yourselves from being punished.

It is very foolish to tell lies; for, soon or late, they are found out; and it is very mean and wicked. God himself has said that we must not lie; that he abhors liars, and that he will punish them.

Section 5.

Do not speak rudely to any body, or quarrel with any body.

Who likes quarrelsome, ill humoured people, or likes to be with them, or takes pains to oblige them? They do not look pleasant and cheerful.

They are not at all happy. They feel quite uncomfortable. They know they do wrong; and they know that the persons who live with them, do not love them, nor wish to oblige them, as they do those who are kind, and civil, and good humoured.

When you are disappointed of any thing you wished for, do not tease people about it, nor fret, nor cry, nor look sullen. Try to think no more of it; and amuse, or please, or employ yourselves, with something else. No persons can have every thing they desire.

Section 6.

When you see very old people, or people who are very ugly, and deformed, do not stare at them, or laugh at them, or mock them.

Though you are now so young and healthy, you may be very sick, and become thin, and pale, and weak, and look very ugly; or you may have a fall, and break your leg or back, and be lame and deformed.

If you live to be old, your hair will become

gray, or fall off; you will lose your teeth; your faces will be covered with wrinkles; you will be very weak, almost like little children; and, perhaps, you will be deaf, and blind, and lame.

Would you, then, like that naughty boys and girls should laugh at you, and play you tricks? No; I am sure you would like that every body should pity you, and be kind to you, and try to help you.

Section 7.

Never amuse yourselves with giving pain to any body, not even to dumb creatures.

A great many animals are killed, because we want their flesh for food; and a great many are killed, because, if we were to let them live, they would do us harm: but I can see no reason that little boys or girls should kill flies, or pull off their wings, or legs; or catch butterflies, and crush them to death; or steal young birds from their soft, warm, comfortable nests; or whip, and beat, horses and asses, till their sides bleed, and are very sore; or do any cruel actions.

The beasts kill one another: wolves kill sheep;

kites, hawks, and eagles, kill little birds; and little birds kill worms and flies: but wolves kill sheep; kites, hawks, and eagles, kill little birds; and little birds kill flies and worms; for food, and not for sport, as some naughty children kill, or torture insects, birds, and beasts. O, it is very cruel sport indeed!

Section 8.

Do not waste any thing. If you have more clothes and food than you want, do not spoil them, or throw them away: but give them, or ask your parents to give them, to poor little boys and girls, who have no clothes scarcely to put on, no meat for dinner, and perhaps no bread and milk for breakfast and supper.

When any body is ill in the house where you live, be very quiet, lest you should disturb them. Do every thing you can to make them well again.

When you are ill yourselves, try to be patient: do not cry, nor be ill humoured to the persons who are so kind as to wait upon you.

Take what is given to you to make you better, without a cross word, or look. Medicines are not pleasant to taste; but they are meant to do you good.

Section 9.

Do not be uncleanly, or untidy, whether you are well, or ill. Keep your hands, and faces, and hair, and every part of your body, quite clean; and your clothes neat, and in good order. It is very unpleasant to look at filthy people, or to be near them.

Children who are kept cleanly and tidy, generally grow much stronger and healthier, and more cheerful and good humoured, than those who are seldom cleaned, and who wear very filthy, ragged clothes.

Section 10.

If the clothes, and the food, that are given you, are proper for you, do not find fault with them; but be thankful for them, though they are not what you like as well as some other things.

Do not eat more than is necessary. Persons who eat too much are called gluttons. They are stupid, and heavy, and idle; and, very often, they have a sad pain in their head, and stomach.

Take care of every thing that belongs to you. If you have drawers of your own, keep them in good order. Persons who always put their things in the proper places, very seldom lose any thing: when they want a thing, they know where to find it; and they need not waste their time in looking for it.

Section 11.

Do not, if you can help it, keep company with children who lie, or steal, or quarrel, or use bad words, lest they should teach you to do as they do; and that people who see you with them, should think, and say, that you too are naughty.

If the people whom you must live with, behave ill, take great care not to learn their bad ways. If they see that you are very good indeed, perhaps they will learn to be like you. Good people should not learn to be like bad people; but bad people should learn to be like good people.

Section 12.

Do not be curious to know what people do **not** wish you to know. Do not look at their letters or what they are writing, unless they give you leave; perhaps there is something in their letters, or what they are writing, which they do not wish you to see.

Do not listen at doors, or in any places where people who are talking, do not see you, or know that you are attending to what they say.

Section 13.

Do as you are bid by those who teach you. Take pains to improve in reading, writing, and whatever else your parents are so kind as to teach you, or wish you to learn.

Do not think you know better than your parents, and your teachers. They have lived a great deal longer than you have; they have read, and seen, and heard, a great many things which you know nothing of. You have lived longer than little infants, and you know more; but great boys and girls know more than you do; and men and women know more than great boys and girls do.

Do not read any books but those which your parents, or teachers, give you leave to read. Some books are not proper for you to read: they are like bad companions; they teach wrong things. It is better not to read at all, than to read bad books.

Section 14.

Our parents are very good to us; but God is better than our parents, and he has done more for us. He gave us our parents, and every thing we have. He is not a man; he is wiser, and better, than any man ever was, or ever can be.

He made the sun, moon, and stars; the earth, and the sky; water, trees, and flowers; birds and beasts, fishes and insects; and men, women, and children.

He has made us more excellent than the beasts; for he has given us a soul. It is our soul that knows God, and that he is good, and wise, and powerful. The beasts do not know God, nor the things which he has made; if we were to tell them, they would not understand us. Our souls learn and know a great many things, which the beasts cannot learn. Our bodies will die like the beasts. When we are laid in the grave, worms will devour our flesh, and our bones will crumble into dust. But our souls are immortal; they will never die.

God orders every thing. He keeps us alive; and he makes us die when he pleases. There is nothing which he cannot do. He sees us wherever we are, by night as well as by day; and he knows all that we do, and say, and think. There is nothing which he does not know.

Section 15.

We must love God. Good people love him more than they love any thing, or any person in the world. They never rise in the morning or lie down at night, without thinking of him, and of the good he has done them. Often in the day, they think of him; and they love to talk, and hear, and read about him.

We must pray to God; that is, we must tell him that we know he is very good, and worthy to be loved; that we hope he will forgive us when we do wrong, put good thoughts into our minds, and help us to be better and better; and that he will bless us, and our parents, and all our kind friends, and give us every good thing that is proper for us.

We must do to all persons what God requires us to do. It is his will that we should not be unkind, even to people who are unkind to us; and that we should do to all persons as we wish they would do to us.

The things that God requires of us will make us good, and happy. If we do them not, he will be displeased with us, and punish us. He can punish us in whatever way he pleases. He can take away all our friends, and every thing that he has given us; and, after death, he can make us very miserable for ever. But if we try to do good, and to do as he would have us to do, he will help us to be good; he will bless us; he will make us feel happy in our minds: and when we die, that is, when our souls leave our bodies, he will take us into heaven; where we shall be with him, and know, and love, and praise him better than any body in this world can know, and love, and praise him. Then we shall never grieve any more; we shall never do wrong any more: we shall be wiser, and happier, than any body who lives here, can be, or can imagine.

Section 16.

We must love to read the Bible. It is the most excellent and beautiful of all books. God himself commanded good men to write it. There, we read of all the great and good things God has done for us, and for all people; how just, and wise, and powerful he is; and what we must do to serve and please him. There, we read of good men who loved God, and whom he loved and blessed; of Abraham, Isaac, and Jacob, of Joseph, Moses, Samuel, and David.

There too, we read of Christ, who was so good, and who has done so much for us. He never did harm to any body; he never did any thing that was wrong. He was gentle and patient when he was troubled, and when he was ill used; he was kind to all persons, even to those who were unkind to him; and when wicked men were just going to kill him, he prayed to God to forgive them.

When we have read, or heard, about Christ, and who he was, and what great things he has done for us, we must love him, and be thankful to him, and try to be like him.

Children, make haste to learn to read, and to understand the meaning of what you read; love to learn your duty, and to do it; then you will be able to read the Bible, and you will love to read it.—There are many things in it which you can understand now, though you are so young. When you are older and wiser, you will understand it better; and if you are good, you will delight in it more and more.

Chapter 6.

Figures and numbers.

	Arabic.	Roman.
One	1	I.
Two	2	II.
Three	3	III.
Four	4	IV.
Five	5	V.
Six	6	VI.
Seven	7	VII.
Eight	8	VIII.
Nine	9	IX.
Ten	10	X.
Eleven	11	XI.
Twelve	12	XII.
Thirteen	13	XIII.
Fourteen	14	XIV.
Fifteen	15	XV.
Sixteen	16	XVI.
Seventeen	17	XVII.
Eighteen	18	XVIII.
Nineteen	19	XIX.
Twenty	20	XX.
Twenty five	25	XXV.

FIGURES AND NUMBERS.

	Arabic.	Roman.
Thirty	30	XXX.
Thirty five	35	XXXV.
Forty	40	XL.
Forty five	45	XLV.
Fifty	50	L.
Fifty five	55	LV.
Sixty	60	LX.
Sixty five	65	LXV.
Seventy	70	LXX.
Seventy five	75	LXXV.
Eighty	80	LXXX.
Eighty five	85	LXXXV.
Ninety	90	XC.
One hundred	100	C.
Two hundred	200	CC.
Three hundred	300	CCC.
Four hundred	400	CCCC.
Five hundred	500	D.
Six hundred	600	DC.
Seven hundred	700	DCC.
Eight hundred	800	DCCC.
Nine hundred	900	DCCCC.
One thousand	1000	M.

P

Chapter 7.

Abbreviations used in writing and printing.

A. B. or B. A. Bachelor of Arts.
ABP. Archbishop.
A. D. In the year of our Lord.
A. M. or M. A. Master of Arts.
A. M. In the year of the world.
A M. Before noon.
P. M. After noon.
B. D. Bachelor of Divinity.
D. D. Doctor of Divinity.
BP. Bishop.
BART. Baronet.
COL. Colonel.
C. S. Keeper of the Seal.
C. P. S. Keeper of the Privy Seal.
ESQ. Esquire.
F. L. S. Fellow of the Linnæan Society.
F. A. S. Fellow of the Antiquarian society.
F. R. S. Fellow of the Royal Society.
G. R. George the King.
HON. Honourable.
J. H. S. Jesus the Saviour of Men.
J. D. Doctor of Law.
KNT. Knight.
LIEUT. Lieutenant.
L. S. Place of the Seal.
L. L. D. Doctor of the Canon and Civil Law.
M. D. Doctor in Physic.
MR. Mister.

MRS. Mistress.
M. S. Sacred to the Memory.
M. P. Member of Parliament.
MS. Manuscript.
MSS. Manuscripts.
N. B. Mark well.
No. Number.
N. S. New Style.
O. S. Old Style.
OXON. Oxford.
PHILOM. A lover of the Mathematics.
PER CENT. By the hundred.
P. M. G. Professor of Music at Gresham college.
P. S. Postscript.
Q. Queen.
REG. PROF. King's Professor.
RT. HON. Right Honourable.
ST. Saint.
S. T. P. Professor of Divinity.
XT. Christ.
XTN. Christian.
ULT. The last.
IB. or IBID. The same place.
ID. The same.
E. G. or V. G. As for example.
I. E. That is.
Q. D. As if he should say.
Q. L. As much as you please.
Q. S. A sufficient quantity.
V. For VIDE. See.
VIZ. For VIDELICET. That is to say.
&. And.
&c. et cetera, and so forth.

Chapter 8.

Reading lessons, in Italic, old English, and manuscript letters.

Section 1.

Italic letters.

A	*B*	*C*	*D*	*E*	*F*	*G*	*H*	*I*
J	*K*	*L*	*M*	*N*	*O*	*P*	*Q*	*R*
S	*T*	*U*	*V*	*W*	*X*	*Y*	*Z*	

a	*b*	*c*	*d*	*e*	*f*	*g*	*h*	*i*
j	*k*	*l*	*m*	*n*	*o*	*p*	*q*	*r*
s	*t*	*u*	*v*	*w*	*x*	*y*	*z*	

Select sentences.

Do to others as you wish they should do to you.

How pleasant it is to live with persons, who are kind, and cheerful, and willing to oblige; who never take, or keep, what does not belong to them; and who always speak the truth!

When you are told of a fault, endeavour to avoid it afterwards.

We must not do wrong, because we see others do so.

Be not afraid to do what is right and proper for you to do.

Never ask other persons to do any thing for you, which you can as properly do for yourselves.

As soon as you have learned to work well, try to work quick.

If we do not take pains, we must not expect to excel in any thing.

Attentive and industrious people, can always find time to do what is proper for them to do.

How comfortable it is to feel that we dearly love our parents, our brothers and sisters, and all our relations and friends; and to know that they love us, and wish to serve us, and make us happy.

Persons who desire to gain knowledge, listen to their instructers with attention and respect.

Ignorant, foolish, and obstinate persons, are very disagreeable to others, and unhappy in themselves.

The Parrots.

Two parrots were confined together in a large cage. The cup which held their food, was put at the bottom of the cage. They commonly sat on the same perch, and close beside each other. Whenever one of them went down for food, the other always followed; and when they had eaten enough, they hastened together to the highest perch of the cage.

They lived four years in this state of confinement; and always showed a strong affection for each other. At the end of this time, the female grew very weak, and had all the marks of old age. Her legs swelled, and she was no longer able to go to the bottom of the cage to take her food: but her companion went and brought it to her. He carried it in his bill, and emptied it into hers.

This affectionate bird continued to feed his mate, in this manner, for four months. But her weakness increased every day. At last she was unable to sit on the perch; and remained crouched at the bottom of the cage. Sometimes she tried to get up to the lower perch, but was not able.

Her companion did all he could to assist her. He often took hold of the upper part of her wing with his bill, and tried to draw her up to him. His looks and his motions showed a great desire to help her, and to make her sufferings less.

But the sight was still more affecting, when the female was dying. Her distressed companion went round and round her a long time, without stopping. He tried at last to open her bill, that he might give her some food. His trouble increased every moment. He went to and from her, with the utmost appearance of distress. Sometimes he made the most mournful cries: at other times, he fixed his eyes on his mate, and was silent; but his looks showed the deepest sorrow. His companion at length died: and this affectionate and interesting bird grew weaker and weaker from that time; and lived only a few months.

This is an affecting lesson, to teach us to be kind, and loving, and very helpful, to one another; and to those persons in particular, who are nearly connected with us, and who stand in need of our assistance.

Section 2.

Old English.

A B C D E F G H
I J K L M N O P Q
R S T U W X Y Z

a b c d e f g h i
j k l m n o p q r
s t u v w x y z

The charitable Sisters.

People who love to serve and oblige others, can find many ways of doing it, which selfish, unkind people do not think of.

Some little girls, who were sisters, and whose parents were rich, had a full glass of good wine allowed them, every day. They said one to another: "We are strong and healthy, we can do without wine. We will, very often, save our wine; and pour it into a bottle, for poor people who are sick. They cannot afford to buy wine, even when the doctor tells them, it would do them more good than any medicines. When we have money, we will give them some money also; or we will buy things for them that they want."

These good little girls did as they said. When they heard that any of their poor neighbours were sick, and that wine would do them good, they were very glad to have a bottle ready for them. The poor people loved them, and were very thankful to them.

When these good children grew up, they had a great deal of time and money to spend as they pleased. Then they saved their wine as they used to do; they worked for poor people; they taught little girls to read, and write, and sew, and gave them books and clothes: and did all the good they could to the poor people whom they knew.

Section 3.

Manuscript.

*A B C D E F G H I
J K L M N O P Q R
S T U V W X Y Z*

*a b c d e f g h i j k l m
n o p q r s t u v w x y z*

The workhouse boy.

A boy, about ten years of age, having lost his father, and his mother being ill at an hospital, was sent to a workhouse*. He behaved well; and worked hard, that he might deserve the food,

---
* At Shrewsbury.

and clothes, and other necessaries, which were allowed him.

Very soon, he had some money given to him, as a reward; and he was told that he might do with the money, just as he pleased. As soon as he had received it, he asked his master's leave to go and see his mother; and he took the money with him, and gave it to her.

O how glad he must have felt, when he gave the money to his mother; it was very little, but it was all he had to give: and how glad she must have been, to have so good a son!

Chapter 9.

Words exactly the same in sound, but different in spelling and signification*.

ALL, every one.
AWL, an instrument to bore holes.
A'L TAR, for sacrifice.
A'L TER, to change.
AIR, one of the elements.
ERE, before.
HEIR, one who inherits.
AS CE'NT, going up.
AS SE'NT, agreement.
AT TE'N DANCE, waiting.
AT TE'N DANTS, waiters.
BARE, naked.
BEAR, a beast.
BEAU, a fop.
BOW, to shoot with.
BEAT, to strike.
BEET, a plant.
BE'R RY, a small fruit.
BU'RY, to lay in the grave.
BEER, malt liquor.
BIER, to carry the dead.
BLEW, did blow.
BLUE, a colour.
BOAR, a beast.
BORE, to make a hole.
BOUGH, a branch.
BOW, to bend.

---

* By associating, in this chapter, such words only as have precisely the same sound, we assist the learner in his pronunciation, as well as enable him to distinguish the meaning of words sounded alike.

WORDS SOUNDED ALIKE.

BREAD, food.
BRED, brought up.
CELL, a hut or cave.
SELL, to dispose of.
SENT, did send.
SCENT, smell.
CEI'L ING, of a room.
SEA'L ING, fixing a seal.
COARSE, not fine.
COURSE, race or way.
CO'M PLE MENT, the full number.
CO'M PLI MENT, civil expression.
DEAR, costly.
DEER, a wild beast.
DEW, on the grass.
DUE, owing.
FAINT, feeble.
FEINT, a pretence.
FAIR, just.
FARE, provisions.
FLEA, an insect.
FLEE, to run from danger.

FOUL, filthy.
FOWL, a bird.
GILT, with gold.
GUILT, sin.
GRATE, for coals.
GREAT, large.
HART, a beast.
HEART, seat of life.
HAIR, of the head.
HARE, a beast.
HEAL, to cure.
HEEL, part of the foot.
HEAR, to hearken.
HERE, in this place.
HEW, to cut.
HUE, colour.
HOLE, a cavity.
WHOLE, total.
KNEW, did know.
NEW, not worn.
LEAK, to run out.
LEEK, an herb.
LEAD, metal.
LED, did lead.

Q

WORDS SOUNDED ALIKE.

LES'SEN, to make less.
LES'SON, a precept.
MEAN, low.
MIEN, appearance.
MEAT, food.
MEET, to assemble.
METE, to measure.
MOAN, to lament.
MOWN, cut down.
OAR, to row with.
ORE, metal.
PAIN, uneasiness.
PANE, square of glass.
PAIR, a couple.
PARE, to cut off.
PEAR, a fruit.
PEACE, quiet.
PIECE, a part.
PEER, a nobleman.
PIER, a column.
PLACE, situation.
PLAICE, a fish.
PRAY, to beseech.
PREY, plunder.

RAISE, to lift up.
RAYS, sun beams.
RAZE, to demolish.
RAIN, from the clouds.
REIGN, to rule.
REIN, of a bridle.
REST, repose.
WREST, to force.
RYE, corn.
WRY, crooked.
RIGHT, just.
RITE, a ceremony.
WRIGHT, an artificer.
WRITE, to use a pen.
SAIL, of a ship.
SALE, selling.
SCENE, the stage.
SEEN, beheld.
SEA, the ocean.
SEE, behold.
SEAM, edges sewed.
SEEM, to appear.
SOW, to scatter seed.
SEW, to work with a needle,

WORDS SOUNDED ALIKE.

SLEIGHT, dexterity.
SLIGHT, to despise.
SLOE, a fruit.
SLOW, tardy.
SOLE, of the foot.
SOUL, spirit.
SOAR, to fly aloft.
SORE, an ulcer.
SOME, a part.
SUM, the whole.
SON, a male child.
SUN, the cause of day.
STEAL, to pilfer.
STEEL, hardened iron.
STILE, a passage.
STYLE, language.
STRAIGHT, not crooked.
STRAIT, narrow.
SU'C COUR, help.
SU'CK ER, a twig.

TAIL, the end.
TALE, a story.
THEIR, of them.
THERE, in that place.
TOO, likewise.
TWO, a couple.
TOE, of he foot.
TOW, of flax.
VALE, a valley.
VEIL, a cover.
VAIN, worthless.
VANE, a weather-cock.
VEIN, a blood vessel.
WAIST, of the body.
WASTE, loss.
WEAK, not strong.
WEEK, seven days.
YEW, a tree.
YOU, yourselves.

Chapter 10.

Words which are often improperly confounded, in spelling or pronunciation, or both.

CE′ LE RY, a species of parsley.
SA′ LA RY, stated hire.

CO′N CERT, harmony.
CO′N SORT, companion.

COU′N CIL, persons met in consultation.
COU′N SEL, advice, direction.

E ME′RGE, to rise, to mount from obscurity.
IM ME′RGE, to put under water.

E′ MI NENT, high, exalted.
IM′ MI NENT, impending, at hand.

GE′ N US, mental power, peculiar disposition.
GE′NUS, class containing many species.

IN GE′ NI OUS, inventive, possessed of genius.
IN GE′ NU OUS, candid, generous.

TO LAY, to place, to quiet.
TO LIE, to be in a reclining posture, to rest.

LI' CO RICE, a root of sweet taste.
LI'CK ER ISH, nice in the choice of food.

OR' DI NANCE, a law or rule.
ORD' NANCE, cannon, great guns.

PE'R SE CUTE, to pursue with malice.
PRO' SE CUTE, to continue, to sue at law.

PRI'N CI PAL, a head, a sum placed at interest.
PRI'N CI PLE, first cause, fundamental truth.

RE' LIC, remainder.
RE' LICT, a widow.

PRE' CE DENT, a rule or example.
PRE' SI DENT, one at the head of others.

STA' TUE, an image.
STA' TUTE, a law.

TE' NOR general course or drift.
TE' NURE, the manner of holding estates.

TRACK, mark left, a road.
TRACT, a country, a quantity of land.

Chapter 11.

Words spelled alike, but which differ in pronunciation and meaning.

CO'N DUCT, management, behaviour.
TO CON DU'CT, to lead, to direct.

A CO'N TEST, a dispute, difference.
TO CON TE'ST, to strive, to contend.

FRE' QUENT, often seen, often occurring.
TO FRE QU'ENT, to visit often.

A MI' NUTE, the sixtieth part of an hour.
MI NU'TE, small, slender.

AN OB' JECT, that on which one is employed.
TO OB JE'CT, to oppose.

A SU'B JECT, one who is governed.
TO SUB JE'CT, to make submissive.

A PRE' SENT, a gift, a donation.
TO PRE SE'NT, to give, to show.

A TO'R MENT, pain, misery.
TO TOR ME'NT, to put to pain, to vex.

A TEAR, water from the eyes.
TO TEAR, to pull in pieces.

A SOW, a female hog.
TO SOW, to scatter seed in the ground.

A BOW, an instrument of war.
TO BOW, to bend the body in respect.

A MOW, a loft where hay or corn is laid up.
TO MOW, to cut with a sithe.

A HOUSE, a place to live in.
TO HOUSE, to harbour, to shelter.

USE, advantage, custom.
TO USE, to employ to any purpose.

CLOSE, shut fast, confined.
TO CLOSE, to shut, to finish.

GREASE, the soft part of the fat.
TO GREASE, to smear with grease.

AN EX CU'SE, an apology.
TO EX CU'SE, to admit an apology*.

---

* The last five pair of words, are distinguished by the *s*, in the first word, being sharp; and, in the second flat, like *z*.

Chapter 12.

Words in which the pronunciation differs remarkably from the spelling.

Spelling.	Pronunciation.	Spelling.	Pronunciation.
AISLE,	Ile.	HA'LF PENCE,	Há pence.
A' PRON,	A' purn.	HAU'T BOY,	Hó boy.
BEAUX,	Boes.	HI'C COUGH,	Híc cup.
BELLE,	Bell.	HOUSE' WIFE,	Húz zif.
BI'S CUIT,	Bís kit.	I' RON,	I' urn.
BOA'T SWAIN,	Bó sen.	LIEU TE' NANT,	Lev tén nant.
BU' RY,	Bér re.	ONE,	Wun.
BU' SY,	Bíz ze.	ONCE,	Wunce.
BU' SI NESS,	Bíz ness.	PHTHI' SIC,	Tíz zic.
CA'T SUP,	Cátch up.	RA GOU'T,	Rag góo.
CO'CK SWAIN,	Cók sn.	SCHE' DULE,	Séd jule.
CO' LO NEL,	Cúr nel.	SCHISM,	Sizm.
CORPS,	Core.	SCHIS' MA TIC,	Síz ma tic.
CU' CUM BER,	Ców cum ber.	SEVEN' NIGHT,	Sén nit.
CU'P BOARD,	Cúb burd.	SUB' TLE,	Sút tle.
CRI TI' QUE,	Crit teék.	TWO,	Too.
E CLA'T,	E cláw.	VI'C TU ALS,	Vít tlz.
EWE,	Yu.	WAI'ST COAT,	Wés kot.
GAOL,	Jail.	WO' MEN,	Wím men.
HA'LF PEN NY,	Há pen ne.	YACHT,	Yot.

Chapter 13.

Words which are often pronounced very erroneously*.

BILE for BOIL.	SARCER for SAUCER.
PINT for POINT.	DIXONARY for DICTIONARY.
PYZON for POISON.	HAIR for AIR.
CHEER for CHAIR.	AIR for HAIR.
KETCH for CATCH.	HARROW for ARROW.
YOURN for YOURS.	ARROW for HARROW.
HERN for HERS.	DROWNDED for DROWNED.
HIZEN for HIS.	NATUR for NATURE.
WEAL for VEAL.	CRETUR for CREATURE.
RENSH for RINSE.	LUNNUN for LONDON.
FIFT for FIFTH.	WINDER for WINDOW.
SIXT for SIXTH.	SITTIATION for SITUATION.
GETHER for GATHER.	EDDICATION for EDUCATION.
KITTLE for KETTLE.	CIRKILATION for CIRCULATION.
SITHE for SIGH.	LIBARY for LIBRARY.
TOWER for TOUR.	WINEGAR for VINEGAR.

---

* Though the manner in which these words, and others of a similar nature, are frequently pronounced, is extremely erroneous, yet as young persons of education, as well as others, are apt to imitate what they hear, it is proper to guard them against so corrupt a pronunciation.

Chapter 14.

Words in which the terminations *ar, er, or, our,* and *re,* have exactly the same sound, viz. that of *ur**.

BEG GAR.	SU GAR.
COL LAR.	VUL GAR.
DOL LAR.	CE DAR.
NEC TAR.	FRI AR.
PIL LAR.	LI AR.
SCHO LAR.	MOR TAR.
DAN GER.	CHAM BER.
GAN DER.	CI DER.
LODG ER.	GRO CER.
SING ER.	SPEAK ER.
SUP PER.	STRAN GER.
USH ER.	WA FER.

---

* Though the words comprised in this chapter, are not numerous, they are perhaps sufficient to excite the learner's attention, both to the orthography and the pronunciation of such words.

SOUNDED ALIKE.

AC TOR.	AU THOR.
DEBT OR.	JU ROR.
DOC TOR.	MAY OR.
LI QUOR.	MI NOR.
MA NOR.	TAI LOR.
PAS TOR.	TRAI TOR.
REC TOR.	TU TOR.
AR MOUR.	SUC COUR.
CAN DOUR.	VA LOUR.
CO LOUR.	VI GOUR.
HAR BOUR.	LA BOUR.
HO NOUR.	FA VOUR.
RAN COUR.	NEIGH BOUR.
SPLEN DOUR.	HU MOUR.
CEN TRE.	ME TRE.
LUS TRE.	MEA GRE.
SCEP TRE.	MI TRE.
SPEC TRE.	NI TRE.
A CRE.	SA BRE.
FI BRE.	SALT PE TRE.
LU CRE.	SE PUL CHRE.

Chapter 15.

Words in which the initial letters *e* and *i* are often misapplied*.

EM BALM.	IM BIT TER.
EM BEZ ZLE.	IM BO DY.
EM PO VE RISH.	IM BOL DEN.
EN CAMP.	IM BO SOM.
EN CHANT.	IM BRUE.
EN CLOSE.	IM BUE.
EN CROACH.	IM PLANT.
EN DITE.	IM PRI SON.
EN DORSE.	IN CREASE.
EN FORCE.	IN CUM BER.
EN GROSS.	IN FLAME.
EN JOIN.	IN GEN DER.
EN LIST.	IN GRAFT.
EN ROLL.	IN QUIRE.
EN SHRINE.	IN SNARE.
EN SURE	IN TRUST.
EN TAIL.	IN TWINE.
EN TREAT.	IN WRAP.

---

* These letters, in the words of this chapter, are properly applied, according to Dr. Johnson's Dictionary.

INTRODUCTION

TO THE SUBSEQUENT CHAPTERS.

The learner has hitherto been occupied with the mere practical part of spelling. It is proper now to present him with a few of the simple rules and principles, by which the practice is governed. They will lead him to reflect, with advantage, on the various powers of the letters, and on the connexion and influence which subsist amongst them: and as they are, in many instances, illustrated by a considerable number of examples, they will be the more intelligible to young minds, and make a stronger impression. In a Spelling-book, to omit rules for spelling; and in a book which teaches pronunciation, to omit rules respecting the sounds of the letters; might justly be deemed very culpable omissions. If these rules are not now, in some degree, inculcated, they will probably, in future, be hastily passed over, if not entirely neglected.

The scholar who has passed through the preceding parts of the book, and been conversant with the nature and sounds of the letters, must certainly, with the teacher's aid, be capable of understanding some of the most simple rules respecting them: especially as the Exercises in the Appendix now added to the work, will render these rules not only easy, but impressive.

We may further observe, that as the rules contained in these chapters, are intended to prepare the scholar for entering on the author's " Abridgment of his English Grammar," this circumstance forms an additional reason for inserting them in the latter part of the spelling book.

In studying this part of the work, it would be advisable, that the learner should, in the first instance, pay attention only to the rules and observations expressed in the larger type. This will give him a general idea of the different subjects; which may be afterwards improved, by a careful perusal of the exceptions and remarks contained in the smaller type. Thus initiated, he will be both qualified and disposed to examine the subject with accuracy, when his studies are more advanced, and his knowledge extended.

Chapter 16.

Explanations of vowels and consonants, syllables and words *.

Section 1.

Letters, syllables, &c.

A letter is the least part of a word.

The letters of the English alphabet, are twenty six.

Letters are divided into vowels and consonants. See page 2.

A vowel can be sounded by itself.

A consonant cannot be sounded distinctly by itself.

A diphthong is two vowels forming but one syllable.

A triphthong is three vowels forming but one syllable: as, *eau* in beau.

---

* An explanation of the terms contained in this chapter, appears to be necessary, to enable the learner to understand many of the subsequent rules and lessons.

A proper diphthong has both the vowels sounded: as, *oi* in voice, *ou* in ounce.

An improper diphthong has but one of the vowels sounded: as, *ea* in eagle, *oa* in boat.

A syllable is so much of a word as can be pronounced at once: as, a, an, ant, bit ter, but ter fly.

Words are sounds, used as signs of our thoughts.

A word of one syllable, is called a monosyllable; a word of two syllables, a dissyllable; a word of three syllables, a trisyllable; and a word of four or more syllables, a polysyllable.

Words of two or more syllables, have an accent on one of the syllables.

Accent signifies that stress of the voice, which is laid on one syllable, to distinguish it from the rest. Thus, in áp ple, the accent is on the first syllable; and in a ríse, it is on the second syllable. The mark placed above the syllable, and which denotes the accent, is also called the accent,

Section 2.

Nouns, pronouns, &c.

A noun or substantive, is the name of any thing: as, sun, moon, stars.

Every word that makes sense of itself, is a noun; as, John, Charles, London: or that takes, *a*, *an*, or *the*, before it; as, a tree, an apple, the sun.

A pronoun is a word used instead of a noun, to avoid repeating the noun: as, I, he, she, they: "Charles is a good boy; *he* obeys his parents, and *he* speaks the truth;" instead of saying, "Charles is a good boy; Charles obeys his parents, and Charles speaks the truth."

An adjective is a word that signifies the quality of a substantive: as, good, bad, tall, short: a good girl, a tall tree.

An adjective may be generally known, by its making sense with the word *thing*, or any particular noun added to it: as, a good thing, a bad thing, a sweet apple.

A verb is a word that signifies being, doing, or suffering: as, I am, she writes, he is beaten.

Any word is a verb, when we can prefix a pronoun to it. Thus, eat, read, play, are verbs; because we can say, I eat, she reads, he plays. A verb is also generally known, by its making sense with the word *to* put before it: as, to eat, to read, to play.

The singular number signifies one object: as, a tree, the house.

The plural number signifies more than one object: as, trees, houses.

Section 3.

Primitive and derivative words.

A primitive word is that which cannot be made a more simple word: as, man, good, sincere.

A derivative word is that which may be made a more simple word: as, manful, goodness, sincerely.

A derivative word is sometimes formed of two distinct words joined together: as, inkhorn, bookcase, tea-table: these are termed compound words. A derivative word is also formed of one word, and a syllable or letter joined to it. When the syllable or letter comes first, it is called an initial; when it comes at the end, it is called a termination: as, kind, unkind; please, displease: love, lovely; health, healthy.

INITIALS.

The initials *un, dis, im, in, ir,* signify the same as not, or without, or want of. Thus, unkind, means not kind; unkindness, want of kindness; dishonest, not honest; dishonesty, without honesty; impatient, not patient; inattentive, not attentive; irregular, not regular.

Mis signifies ill, or wrong: as, mismanage, to manage ill; miscall, to name improperly; misbehaviour, bad behaviour.

Re sometimes means backwards, and sometimes it means again: as, return, to turn, or come back; remind, to bring to mind again; recall, to call again, to call back.

TERMINATIONS.

The terminations *ar, er, or,* show the person who makes or does the thing: as, hat, hatter, one who makes hats; beg, beggar, one who begs; collect, collector, one who collects.

Er and *est,* signify comparison: as, wise, wiser, wisest; big, bigger, biggest.

Est, eth, ed, edst, ing, are added to verbs; and some of them give the verbs a different meaning; as, I love, thou lovest, he loveth; she loved, thou lovedst, I am loving.

Ly signifies likeness, or in what manner: as, man, manly, like a man; kind, kindly, in a kind manner.

Y shows a quality or property, in a great degree: as, health, healthy, having health; wood, woody, abounding with wood.

Ish signifies likeness, or a small degree of resemblance: as, child, childish, like a child; white, whitish, rather white.

Full signifies plenty, or abundance: as, joy, joyful, full of joy. This termination is now always spelled with a single *l*.

Less signifies want, or being without: as, care, careless, without care: thought, thoughtless, without thought.

Chapter 17.

The sounds of the letters, with rules to distinguish them.

Section I.

Sounds of the vowels.

Each of the vowels has a long and a short sound. Some of them have also a middle, or a broad sound; and all of them, irregular sounds. We shall consider them under these five divisions.

FIRST, the long sound of the vowels.

All the vowels are sounded long, in the two following cases.

1st. In words or syllables that end with a single consonant and silent *e*: as,

cake	here	mile	bone	fume
name	these	time	rope	pure
tamely	fineness		useful	

EXCEPTIONS.

In *a*: as, are, bade, have; and most words ending in *age*: as, cabbage, village, &c.

In *e*: as, were.

In *o*: as, gone, shone, dove, love, glove, shove, done, none, some, come.

In *i*: as, give, live; and many words ending in *ive* and *ite*: as, narrative, favourite, &c.

Those words or syllables that contain the sounds of the middle vowels, are also excepted: as, gape, move, prude, &c. See pages 192, 193.

2d. At the end of monosyllables, the vowel, when sounded, is long: as, he, me, thy, my, so, no. The middle vowels are excepted: as, ha! do, to, &c. and the broad vowel in la!

SECOND, the short sound of the vowels.

All the vowels have a short sound in the two following cases.

1st. In monosyllables that end with one or more consonants: as,

| Hat | led | fit | not | but |
| cast | bend | dish | long | curl |

EXCEPTIONS.

In *i*: words in which *ld, nd, ght,* follow the vowel: as,

| mild | mind | might |
| child | blind | right |

In *o*: as,

droll	ford	fort	host	torn
roll	sword	port	most	worn
scroll	…….	sport	post	sworn:

and all words, in which *ld* and *lt* follow the vowel: as,

| bold | gold | bolt | dolt |
| cold | sold | colt | jolt |

Those words which contain the sounds of the middle and broad vowels are also excepted: as, balm, bath, ball, bald, &c. See pages 192, 193, 194.

2d. The vowel is also short, in monosyllables that end with two consonants and silent *e*: as,

| chance | hedge | mince | lodge | drudge |
| dance | wedge | hinge | dodge | grudge |

EXCEPTIONS.

In *a*: as, all words in which *st*, *ng*, or *th*, are placed before the silent *e*: as,

        haste   change   bathe
        paste   strange   lathe

In *o*: as, force   forge   bore

These rules for determining when the vowel is long or short, seem to be all that will probably be useful to young learners. Other rules have, however, been advanced by grammarians, namely; The vowel is long, when it ends a syllable; or when the accent rests on the vowel: it is short, when a consonant ends the syllable; or when the accent rests on the consonant. But how is the child to know, when a vowel or a consonant ends the syllable; or when the accent rests on the vowel or the consonant? To tell him, that the vowel ends the syllable, and the accent rests on it, when the vowel is long, &c., would be to argue in a circle, and would not convey to him any satisfactory information.

THIRD, the middle sounds of the vowels *a, o, u.*

A has its middle sound in the following cases.

1st. When it comes before *r* in monosyllables: as, bar, carp, mark, start.

But if *r* be doubled, to form another syllable, the *a* is short: as carry, marry, tarry.

2d. When it is followed by *lm:* as, calm, palm, psalm: except qualm.

3d. When it is followed by *lf, lve,* or by *th* sharp: as, calf, half, salve; bath, lath, path: except hath, wrath.

O has its middle sound, in the following words: prove, move, do, ado, lose, and their compounds; and in who, whom, womb, tomb, Rome, poltron, ponton, &c.

U has its middle sound in the following words.

In bull, pull, full; and in all their compounds: as, bullock, fulfil, delightful, &c.

In puss, push, bush, pullet, bushel, pulpit, bullion, butcher, cushion, cuckoo, pudding, sugar, huzza.

FOURTH, the broad sound of *a*, as in *all*.

A has its broad sound in the following cases.

1st. When it is followed by *ll:* as, all, call, fall, tall, small: except, mall, shall.

2. When it is followed by one *l* and another consonant: as, salt, bald, false.

If the *l* is followed by *p, b, f,* or *v,* the *a* is not broad: as, alps, calf, salve, &c.

3d. When it follows *w,* and precedes *r*: as war, wart, swarm.

4th. In words derived from monosyllables ending in *ll*: as, albeit, almost, also.

When *l* ends one syllable, and begins the next, the *a* is not broad: as, alley, valley, tally

FIFTH. Irregular sounds of the vowels, deviating from their sounds in the scale at page 5.

A.

A sounds like *e* short, in the following words: any, many, Thames, says, said.

A sounds like *i* short, in many words ending in *age,* when the accent is not on it: as, cabbage, village, courage.

E.

E sounds like *a* long, in these words: there, where, ere.

E sounds like middle *a*, in these words: clerk, clerkship, serjeant.

E sounds like *i* short, in these words: yes, pretty, England; and in many final unaccented syllables: as, faces, praises, linen, duel.

E sounds like short *u*, in her: and in the unaccented termination *er*: as, writer, reader, suffer, garter.

I.

I sounds like *e* long, in many words derived from foreign languages: as,

antique	routine	magazine
Brazil	fatigue	marine
caprice	intrigue	police
chagrin	invalid	profile
quarantine	machine	recitative

I sounds like *u* short, when it comes before *r* followed by another consonant: as, bird, dirt, thirst.

I sounds like *e* short, in the following words; which are exceptions to the preceding rule:

| birth | gird | girt | skirt |
| firm | girl | mirth | whirl |

O.

O generally sounds like *a* broad, when it is followed by *r*: as,

| morn | horn | adorn | for |
| scorn | thorn | exhort | formerly |

O sounds like short *u*, in many words: as,

monk	some	among	comfort
month	ton	brother	covenant
shove	worm	colour	Somerset

U.

U sounds like short *e*, in these words: bury, burial, burier.

U sounds like short *i*, in these words; busy, busily, business, busybody.

U sounds like middle *o*, in these words:

| crude | rule | brute | prune | spruce |
| rude | Ruth | prude | truth | truce |

Section 2.

General sounds of the principal diphthongs.

OI, OU, &c.

Oi and *oy* have both the vowels sounded: as, boil, toil, soil; boy, coy, toy.—The sound of these diphthongs, is that of broad *a* and long *e*.

Ou and *ow* have both the vowels sounded: as, mouse, spout, trout: cow, vow, town.—The sound of these diphthongs, is that of broad *a* and middle *u*.

EXCEPTIONS.

Ou is sometimes sounded like short *u* : as, rough, touch, courage.

Sometimes like middle *o* : as, group, soup, surtout.

Sometimes like *o* long : as, court, mould, shoulder.

Ow is sometimes sounded like *o* long : as, blow, crow, snow.

AI, EI, &c.

Ai, ay, ei, and *ey* are sounded like *a* in *fate*: as,

pail	day	vein	prey
sail	say	eight	they
tail	way	weight	obey

EXCEPTIONS.

Ai is sometimes sounded like *a* short : as, plaid, raillery.

Sometimes like *e* short : as, said, again, against.

Sometimes like *i* short, as when it is in a syllable not accented : as, fountain, captain, curtain.

Ei sometimes sounds like long *e* : as, either, neither, ceiling, deceit, receive.

Sometimes like long *i* : as, height, sleight.

Sometimes like short *i*, as when it is not accented : as, foreign, forfeit, surfeit.

Ey, when unaccented, sounds like long *e* : as, alley, barley, valley.

EA, EE, IE.

Ea, ee, and *ie* have the long sound of *e :* as,

bean	beer	chief
cream	feet	grief
please	steel	believe

EXCEPTIONS.

Ea is frequently sounded like short *e* : as, bread, dead, spread.

Sometimes like middle *a* : as, heart, hearth, hearken.

Ee is sounded like short *i*, in the word breeches.

Ie is sometimes sounded like long *i* : as, die, lie, pie.

OA, OE.

Oa and *oe* have the long sound of *o:* as, boat, coat, loaf; doe, foe, toe.

EXCEPTION.

Oe sounds like middle *o*, in shoe, and canoe: and like short *u* in does.

EU, &c.

Eu, ew, and *ue* have the long sound of *u:* as, feud, deuce; dew, new, few; clue, blue, hue.

EXCEPTIONS.

Ew is sounded like long *o*, in the word sew.

Ew, when preceded by *r*, sounds like middle *o*; as, brew, crew, drew.

Ue is sometimes sounded like short *e*: as, guess, guesser, guest.

After *r*, it has the sound of middle *o*: as, rue, true, imbrue.

AU, AW.

Au and *aw* are sounded like *a* broad: as, Paul, taught, caught; law, bawl, crawl.

EXCEPTIONS.

Au, when followed by *n* and another consonant, has the sound of middle *a*: as, aunt, haunt, launch.

In laugh and draught, it also sounds like middle *a*.

In cauliflower, laurel, and laudanum, it sounds like short *o*. And in gauge, like long *a*.

OO.

Oo has the sound of middle *o*: as, food, soon, moon.

EXCEPTIONS.

Oo, before *k*, sounds like middle *u*: as, book, cook, look, and in the following words*:

| foot | good | wool | withstood |
| hood | wood | stood | understood |

Section 3.

Sounds of the consonants.

C.

C is sounded hard, like *k*, before *a*, *o*, and *u*: as, card, cord, curd.

C is sounded soft, like *s*, before *e*, *i*, and *y*: as, cedar, city, cyprus.

C sounds like *z*, in suffice, discern, sacrifice.

C has the sound of *sh*, in ocean, special, delicious, &c.

D.

D frequently sounds like *t*, in the abbreviated

---
* See the note at page 28.

termination *ed*: as, stuffed, rasped, cracked, hissed, touched, faced, mixed; pronounced, stuft, raspt, crackt, &c.

D sounds like *j*, in soldier, grandeur, verdure, education.

G.

G is sounded hard before *a, o, u, l,* and *r*: as, game, gone, gull, glory, grandeur.

G is sounded soft, before *e, i,* and *y*: as, gelly, gipsy, elegy: except in get, giddy, foggy; and some others.

Q.

Q has the sound of *k*, and is always accompanied by *u*, which generally sounds like *w*: as, quack, quality.

S.

S has a sharp hissing sound at the beginning of words: as, so, sell, sun.

It has the sharp sound after, *f, k, p, t*: as, muffs, socks, lips, mats.

S has a flat buzzing sound like *z*, after *b, d, g,* hard, or *v*: as, ribs, heads, rags, doves.

It is pronounced like *z*, in *as, is, his, was, these,*

those; and in all plurals when the singulars end in a vowel: as, commas, shoes, ways, news.

S sometimes sounds like *sh*: as, sure, sugar, expulsion, dimension, reversion.

S has also the sound of *zh*: as, pleasure, evasion, confusion.

T.

T has three sounds: 1st. that which is heard in tatter, tittle; 2nd. the sound of *tch*: as, nature, fortune, virtue: 3d. the sound of *sh*: as, nation, formation.

X.

X has a sharp sound, like *ks*, when it ends a syllable with the accent on it: as, exercise, excellence.

It is also sounded sharp when the accent is on the next syllable beginning with a consonant: as, excuse, expense.

X has its flat sound like *gz*, when the accent is not on it, and the following accented syllable begins with a vowel: as, exert, exist, example.

X at the beginning of words, has the sound of *z*: as, Xerxes, Xenophon.

Y.

Y, as a consonant, has always the same sound. As a vowel, it has different sounds. When it follows a consonant, and ends a word or syllable, it is pronounced like *i* long, if the accent is on it: as, deny: but like *e* long, if the accent is not on it: as, folly.

CH.

CH has three sounds.

The first like *tch:* as, child, chair, rich.

The second like *sh*, after *l* or *n:* as, filch, bench, and in words from the French: as, chaise, machine.

The third like *k:* as, echo, scholar, stomach.

GH.

GH is frequently pronounced like *f*: as, laugh, cough, enough.

PH.

PH is generally pronounced like *f*: as, phantom, physic, philosophy.

It sounds like *v*, in nephew and Stephen.

The remaining consonants have the sounds, expressed in the table of the elementary sounds, at page 6.

Chapter 18.

The silent letters, with rules denoting them.

Section 1.

Silent vowels.

E.

When the verbal termination *ed* is not preceded by *d* or *t*, the *e* is almost universally silent: as, loved, filled, barred, bribed, saved, nailed: which are pronounced as if written, lovd, filld, barrd, &c.

When *d* or *t* precedes *ed*, the *e* is fully pronounced: as, added, divided, commanded; waited, diverted, translated.

Adjectives ending in *ed* retain the sound of *e*: as, learned, blessed, aged, naked, wicked, scabbed, crooked, forked, wretched, crabbed, ragged, rugged.

When a syllable is added to words which drop the *e*, the *ed*, in those words, has its full and distinct sound: as, reserved, reservedly, reservedness; feigned, feignedly; confused, confusedly.

In words ending in *le* preceded by a consonant, the *e* is not sounded: as, ancle, candle, probable.

SILENT LETTERS.

E before *l,* in a final unaccented syllable, is silent in the following words:

ravel	shrivel	hazel
shekel	swivel	navel
snivel	shovel	weasel
drivel	grovel	

In all other words the *e* before *l,* must be distinctly sounded.

E before *n,* in a final unaccented syllable, and not preceded by *l, m, n,* or *r,* is silent: as, loosen, hearken, harden, heaven.

EXCEPTIONS.

Aspen	kitchen	patten
chicken	leaven	sloven
hyphen	marten	sudden
jerken	mitten	ticken

E is silent at the end of a word or syllable, in which there is another vowel: as, base, basely; tame, tameness; sedate, repose, refuse.

The final *e* silent, serves to lengthen the sound of the preceding vowel: as, can, cane; not, note; past, paste; and to soften the sound of *c* and *g*; as, lac, lace; rag, rage; sing, singe.

I silent.

I is silent, in the words, evil, devil, cousin, business: and generally in the terminations *tion, tient*, &c. pronounced *shun*, *shent*, &c. See page 104.

O.

O, in the termination *on*, after a consonant, is generally silent: as,

| Beacon | pardon | button |
| crimson | parson | weapon |

In *on*, preceded by *l*, *m*, *n*, or *r*, the *o* is sounded: as, melon, sermon, cannon, baron.

UE.

The diphthong *ue* preceded by *g*, or *q*, at the end of words, is silent: as,

Rogue	colleague	catalogue
plague	intrigue	dialogue
Cinque	mosque	opaque
pique	oblique	grotesque

Section 2.
Silent consonants.
B.

When *b* follows *m*, in the same syllable, it is silent: as, numb, benumb, hecatomb.

B is also silent in the words debt, doubt, subtle; and their compounds, debtor, doubtful, doubtless, &c.

C.

C preceded by *s*, and followed by *e* or *i*, is silent: as, scene, scent, sceptre, science.

C is silent in czar, czarina, muscle.

D.

D is silent in handsome, handsel, groundsel.

G.

G, before *n*, in the same syllable, is silent: as, gnat, gnaw, design, foreign.

Gn, at the end of an accented syllable, gives the preceding vowel a long sound: as, condign, oppugn.

Gh is generally silent at the end of a word or syllable, or when followed by *t*: as,

    Although   brightly   delightful

Gh lengthens the preceding vowel.

H.

H is silent at the beginning of the following words, and their derivatives: but in every other word it is sounded.

Heir	hour	honour	humble
herb	honest	hostler	humour.

H is always silent after *r*: as, rhubarb, rhetoric, rheumatism.

H final, preceded by a vowel, is always silent: as, ah! oh! Hannah, hallelujah, Messiah.

K.

K is always silent before *n*, in the same syllable: as, knit, knuckle, knowledge.

Ck, at the end of words and syllables, sounds like *k* only; and the preceding vowel is short: as, stock, packet, pocket.

L.

L, between *a* and *k* in the same syllable, is silent: as, balk, chalk, stalk.

L, between *a* and *m* in the same syllable, is also silent: as, alms, balm, psalm.

L is also silent in the following words: calf, halve, could, would, should, falcon, chaldron, salmon, malmsey.

N.

N, preceded by *m*, is silent, when it ends a syllable: as,

Hymn	column	condemn
solemn	autumn	contemn

P.

P, between *m* and *t* in the middle of words, or in a final syllable, is silent: as, empty, redemption; attempt, contempt, exempt.

P is also silent in psalm, psalmist, psalter, pshaw, receipt, raspberry, sempstress.

S.

S is silent in isle, island, aisle, viscount.

T.

T is silent, when preceded by *s,* and followed by the abbreviated terminations *en* and *le*: as,

Hasten	thistle	castle
listen	epistle	bristle
moisten	apostle	bustle.

T is also silent in the following words:

Often	Christmas	mortgage
soften	chestnut	bankruptcy
currant	hostler	mistletoe.

W.

W is always silent before *r*: as, wren, wrestle, wrinkle.

It is also silent before *h* followed by long or middle *o*: as, whole, who, whose.

Chapter 19.

Rules for spelling.

Section 1.

Rules for the division of syllables.

RULE I.—A single consonant between two vowels, must be joined to the latter syllable: as, be have, de sire, re main; pa per, du ty, ci ty; a cid, magic, ta cit; a wake, hea vy, sea son; ge ne ral, mi se ry, ca pa ci ty.

EXCEPTIONS.

The letter *x* is always joined to the first syllable: as, ex alt, ex ist, lux u ry *.

Some derivative words are also exceptions: as, up on, un even, dis use, pri son er, &c.

RULE II.—Two consonants, proper to begin a syllable†, must not be separated, if the preceding vowel is long: as, ta ble, de clare, o blige, nee dle.

If the preceding syllable is short, the consonants must be separated: as, cus tard, pub lic, gos ling.

---

* As *w* or *y*, at the end of a syllable, is a vowel, it forms no exception to the first rule: as, tow el, roy al.

† The consonants which are proper to begin a syllable, may be seen in the section of syllables at pages 11, 12.

EXCEPTIONS.

A few words, in which the consonants are preceded by a short, must be excepted: as, a fraid, a gree, pa trol, pa tri mo ny, pro ba ble, mi ra cle, &c.

RULE III.—If the two consonants cannot begin a syllable, they must be separated: as, up per, blossom, cot tage; un der, chim ney, mon key.

RULE IV.—When three consonants meet in the middle of a word, they are not to be separated, if they can begin a syllable, and the preceding vowel is long: as, de stroy, re strain, de scribe.

If the preceding syllable is short, the consonants must be separated: as, dis creet, dis tract, dis-train.

RULE V.—When three or four consonants, not proper to begin a syllable, meet between two vowels, such of them as can begin a syllable belong to the latter, the rest to the former syllable: as, ap ply, im prove, in struct, but cher, slaugh ter, hand some; trans gress, post script, parch ment.

RULE VI.—Two consonants which form but one sound, are never separated: as, e cho, fa ther, pro phet, an chor, bi shop. They are to be considered as a single letter.

Rule VII.—Two vowels, not being a diphthong, must be separated into syllables: as, po et, vi al, fu el, so ci e ty.

A diphthong immediately preceding a vowel, is to be separated from it: as, roy al, pow er, jew el.

All the preceding rules refer to primitive words, and are to be considered as operating upon them only. Thus, but cher, slaugh ter, laugh ter, pro phet, are properly divided, as primitives; whilst scorch es, poach er, laugh er, pri son er, have a regular division, as derivatives.

Rule VIII.—In derivative words, the additional syllables are separated: as, sweet er, sweet est, sweet ly; learn ed, learn eth, learn ing; dis like, mis lead, un even; call ed, roll er, dress ing; gold en, bolt ed; be liev er, pleas ing.

EXCEPTIONS.

When the derivative word doubles the single letter of the primitive, one of those letters is joined to the termination: as, beg, beg gar; fat, fat ter; bid, bid ding.

When the additional syllable is preceded by *c* or *g* soft, the *c* or *g* is added to that syllable: as, of fen ces, cot ta ges, pro noun cer, in dul ging; ra cer, fa cing, spi ced; wa ger, ra ging, pla ced; ran ger, chan ging, chan ged.

When the preceding single vowel is long, the consonant, if single, is joined to the termination: as, ba ker, ba king; ho ping, bro ken; po ker, bo ny; wri ter sla vish; mu sed sa ved.

The termination *y* is not to be placed alone: as, san dy, gras sy; dir ty, dus ty; mos sy, fros ty; hea dy, woo dy: except, dough y, snow y, string y, and a few other words. But even in these exceptions, it would be proper to avoid beginning a line with the termination *y*.

RULE IX.—Compounded words must be divided by the simple words which form them: as, black-bird, sea horse, hot house, York shire.

The preceding rules are conformable to the best authorities for the division of syllables. They are definite, and easily applied to every word. Some writers, however, have deviated from the first rule, with a view to assist pronunciation. But the principle of associating letters, according to the pronunciation, may, doubtless, be too far extended. Of this opinion are Nares, Walker, and many other writers. Such a division, besides being contrary to long established practice, would give to a great number of words a most uncouth and perplexing appearance. This may be seen in a few instances: cit y, ver y, mon ey, ac ute, ac id, mag ic, ar ise, av oid, am ong, heav y, troub le, cod le, par as ol, aq uat ic, ap ol o gy, ac ad em y.

The first rule, as it stands in this section, presents the words in neat and regular divisions; and is so far from being affected by an ever varying pronunciation, that it has some tendency to check that variation.—See the opinions in the Reviews cited at the end of this work, particularly the Imperial Review, the British Critic, and the Monthly Review.

Rule x.—The letters, or terminations, *ion, tion, tial, tious, scious, science,* &c. are to be divided into two syllables: as, pil li on, ac ti on, par ti al, cau ti ous, pre ci ous, con sci ence.

The author's reasons in support of the tenth rule, are the following.

1. The rapid pronunciation of two syllables, so as to resemble the sound of one syllable, does not, in fact, make them one. The words business, colonel, victuals, ashamed, believed, &c. are pronounced as two syllables, though they are really three.

2. The division adopted renders the gradations in spelling a word, more simple, and much easier to the learner, than combining the letters. If spelling is made practicable and easy to children, by dividing words into syllables, it follows, that the more this division can be conveniently extended, the better is it calculated to answer the end.

3. The old plan of dividing these letters, or terminations, is uniform and invariable: the new plan, of not dividing them, is liable to numerous exceptions and frequent variations.

4. Combining or separating syllables according to the pronunciation, would present still more irregular and uncouth appearances, than the association of letters, vowels, and consonants, to suit the pronunciation. The following are a few specimens: on ion, o cean, ven geance, pon iard, court ier, scutch eon, bril liant ly, per fid ious ly, punc til io, jus ti ciar y.

5. If the combinations of letters pronounced as one syllable, were to have a correspondent arrangement, we should have an extremely difficult, as well as an extremely irregular, mode of dividing our words into syllables. How would the advocates for dividing according to the pronunciation, divide the words, business, colonel, victuals, sevennight, double, triple, moved, stuffed, devoured, abused, and many others of a similar nature? A rule which, at best, is so inconvenient, and which, in numerous instances, cannot be reduced to practice, certainly does not merit adoption.

6. The best authorities, as well as a great majority of them, may be adduced in support of this division. Walker, in the last edition of his dictionary, says, " Though *tion* and *sion* are really pronounced in one syllable, they are, by almost all our Orthöepists, divided into two; and consequently nation, pronunciation, occasion, evasion, &c. contain the same number of syllables as, natio, pronunciatio, occasio, evasio, in Latin."

On the whole, we think that the old plan, whilst it possesses so much superiority, is liable to no inconvenience. Even pronunciation is as readily acquired by it, as by the new plan. The learner cannot know that *tion* sounds like *shun*, *tial* like *shal*, *science* like *shense*, &c. till his teacher directs him to this pronunciation: and the same direction will teach him that *ti on*, *ti al*, *sci ence*, &c. have the same sounds. Much therefore is lost, and nothing gained, by the new division.

Section 2.

Rules respecting the double consonants, in primitive words.

RULE I.—Monosyllables ending with *f, l*, or *s*, preceded by a single vowel, double the final consonant: as, muff, hill, puss.

EXCEPTIONS.

If	as	has	yes	his	us
of	is	gas	this	was	thus

RULE II.—Monosyllables ending with any consonant but *f, l*, or *s*, preceded by a single vowel, never double the final consonant: as, fib, mud, rug, sun, cur, nut.

EXCEPTIONS.

ebb	odd	inn	err	butt
add	egg	bunn	purr	buzz

RULE III.—A consonant preceded by a diphthong, or a long vowel, is never doubled: as,

ready	couple	laurel	wafer
steady	double	flourish	poker

RULE IV.—Primitive words of more than one syllable, never end with double *l*: as,

Dial	flannel	gambol	annul
frugal	pupil	symbol	mogul

RULE V.—V, x, and k, are never doubled *.

C is used before k, when a single vowel precedes: as, back, neck, pocket, knuckle. At the end of words of two or more syllables, the k is omitted by most writers: as, mimic, public, almanac.

RULE VI.—In dissyllables, the consonant is doubled, when it is preceded by a short vowel, and followed by the termination *le:* as, bubble, saddle, apple, kettle.

Codle, frizle, treble, triple, are frequently given as exceptions: but it would be better, if they were comprehended in the rule.

RULE VII.—In dissyllables ending in *y* or *ey*, the preceding consonant is always doubled, when it follows a short vowel; as, folly, sorry, valley.

EXCEPTIONS.

In y ;	body	any	copy	busy
	study	many	very	city
	lily	cony	bury	pity
In ey ;	honey	money.		

RULE VIII.—In words ending with er, et, ow, the preceding consonant is always doubled, when it follows a short vowel: as, flatter, linnet, tallow.

---

* The third and fifth rules apply also to derivative words.

U

EXCEPTIONS.

In er; primer, proper, choler, soder, leper, consider.
In et; claret closet comet
cadet planet spinet
tenet valet alphabet
In ow; shadow, widow.

RULE IX.—In words ending with ic, id, it, ish, ity, the preceding consonant is never doubled: as, frolic, solid, habit, astonish, quality.

EXCEPTIONS.

In ic; attic, traffic, tyrannic.
In id; horrid, torrid, pallid, flaccid.
In it; rabbit, summit, commit.
In ish; skittish, embellish.
In ity; necessity.

RULE X.—In words beginning with ac, af, ef, of, the consonant, followed by a vowel, is always doubled: as, accord, afford, effect, office.

EXCEPTIONS.

In ac; acute, acumen, acid, academy, acanthus, acerbity.
In af; afore, afar.

RULE XI.—In words beginning with am, cat, el, ep, mod, par, the consonant is never doubled: as, amend, catalogue, elegant, epitaph, modest, paradise.

EXCEPTIONS.

In am; ammoniac, ammunition.
In cat; cattle.
In el; ellipsis.
In par; parry, parrot, parricide.

Further rules for doubling consonants, founded on other initials and terminations, might be inserted: but as they extend to only a few words, or have many exceptions, they are omitted. Those which are mentioned, are explicit and useful, adapted to the limits of this work, and calculated to lead the scholar to further reflections on the subject.

Section 3.

Rules respecting derivative words.

THE orthography of the English language would be simplified and improved, if the rules for spelling derivative words, were uniformly observed. Dr. Johnson seems to have been sensible of this, though he has not paid all the attention to it that is desirable. Many of the inconsistences, or rather contradictions, with respect to derivative words, that occur in his excellent dictionary, arose, probably, from mere inadvertence in himself or his printer. Thus, irreconcilable, immovable, immovably, are spelled according to the general rule; (Rule 2;) whilst reconcileable, moveable, and moveably, are contrary to it. Fertileness and chastely, conform to the general rule; (Rule 3;) fertily, and chastness, deviate from it. Sliness is according to the general rule; (Rule 4;) slyly is contrary to it. Fearlessly, and needlessness, are agreeable to the general rule; (6;) needlesly, and fearlesness, vary from it.—In stating the following rules for spelling derivative words, we have not followed these irregularities. No exceptions are remarked, but those which are supported by long and established custom, or which, from the nature and construction of the language, are absolutely necessary.

RULE I.—The plural number of nouns is formed by adding *s* to the singular: as, pea, peas; table, tables; window, windows; muff, muffs; face, faces*.

EXCEPTIONS.

EXCEP. 1. Nouns ending in x, ss, sh, and ch soft, form the plural number, by the addition of *es*: as,

Tax	taxes	fish	fishes
ass	asses	watch	watches.

---

* In words, in which *e* mute is preceded by the letter c, g, s, or z, the plural number has a syllable more than the singular: as, lace, laces; cage, cages; praise, praises; prize, prizes.

Excep. 2. Nouns ending in *o* form the plural, by adding *es*: as,

Cargo	cargoes	buffalo	buffaloes
echo	echoes	potato	potatoes
hero	heroes	volcano	volcanoes

Those words, in which *i* precedes *o*, follow the general rule, by adding *s* only, to form the plural: as, nuncio, nuncios; punctilio, punctilios; seraglio, seraglios.

Excep. 3.—Nouns ending in *y*, preceded by a consonant, form the plural, by changing *y* into *ies*: as,

Fly	flies	lady	ladies
city	cities	berry	berries

Nouns ending in *y*, preceded by a vowel, follow the general rule, by adding *s* only, to form the plural: as,

Boy	boys	delay	delays
key	keys	attorney	attorneys

Excep. 4.—The following nouns ending in *f*, or *fe*, form the plural number by changing those terminations into *ves*: as,

Calf	calves	self	selves
elf	elves	sheaf	sheaves
half	halves	shelf	shelves
knife	knives	thief	thieves
leaf	leaves	wife	wives
life	lives	wolf	wolves
loaf	loaves		

All other words, ending in *f* or *fe*, follow the general rule.

Excep. 5.—The plural number of the following nouns, is very irregularly formed.

Man	men	mouse	mice
woman	women	louse	lice
child	children	tooth	teeth
goose	geese	foot	feet
ox	oxen	penny	pence

Rule ii.—When a word ending in *e* mute, has a termination added to it, which begins with a vowel, the *e* mute is dropped : as,

Wise	wiser	desire	desirous
noble	noblest	contrive	contrivance
stone	stony	arrive	arrival
white	whiten	manage	manager
pale	palish	place	placing
blame	blamable	divide	divided

EXCEPTIONS.

Words ending in *ce* or *ge*, having *ous* or *able* added to them, retain the *e* mute, to preserve the soft sound of *c* and *g:* as, peace, peaceable; change, changeable; courage, courageous.

Words ending in *ee*, retain both these letters, when *ing* or *able* is added : as, seeing, agreeing, agreeable.

Words ending in *ie*, change *ie* into *y*, before *ing* : as die, dying; lie, lying; tie, tying.

RULE III.—When a word ending in *e* mute, has a termination added to it, which begins with a consonant, the *e* mute is retained: as,

false	falsely	falsehood
fine	finely	fineness
improve		improvement

EXCEPTIONS.

Awe	awful	abridge	abridgment
due	duly	argue	argument
true	truly	judge	judgment
whole	wholly	lodge	lodgment
acknowledge		acknowledgment	

Words ending in *le*, preceded by a consonant, omit *le*, when the termination *ly* is added: as, idle, idly; noble, nobly; gentle, gently; instead of idlely, noblely, gentlely.

RULE IV.—When a termination is added to a word ending in *y*, preceded by a consonant, the *y* is changed into *i*: as,

Try	trial	comply	compliance
envy	envious	justify	justifiable
Happy	happier	happiest	happily
carry	carrier	carrieth	carried

When *ing* is added to such words, the *y* is retained, that the *i* may not be doubled: as, cry, crying; fly, flying,

Words ending in *y* preceded by a vowel, do not change the *y* into *i*: as, gay, gayly; play, played; employ, employer.

When *ed* or *es* is added to a word ending in *y*, it forms but one syllable with the preceding consonants: as, try, tried; deny, denies.

Rule v.—Monosyllables, and words accented on the last syllable, ending with a single consonant preceded by a single vowel, double that consonant, when they take another syllable beginning with a vowel: as, fog, foggy; admit, admittance.

Thin	thinner	thinnest	thinnish
rob	robber	robbed	robbing
begin	beginner	beginneth	beginning
forbid	forbidder	forbidden	forbidding

EXCEPTIONS.

When the additional syllable alters the original accent, the consonant is not doubled: as, confér, cónference, deference, inference, reference, preference, preferable.

Words ending in *l*, preceded by a single vowel, having terminations added to them, beginning with a vowel, generally double the *l*, whether the last syllable is accented, or not accented: as,

| travel | traveller | travelled | travelling |
| distil | distiller | distilled | distilling |

But in words with the terminations *ous, ize, ist,* and *ity,* the *l* is not doubled: as, scandalous, moralize, loyalist, morality: except in the following instances; libellous, marvellous, duellist, tranquillity.

In woolly and woollen, the *l,* though preceded by a diphthong, is doubled.

RULE VI.—Words ending in double consonants, retain both letters, when any termination is added: as,

Odd	oddest	oddly	oddness
stiff	stiffest	stiffly	stiffness
roll	roller	rolled	rolling
possess	possessor	possessed	possessing

EXCEPTION.

Words ending with double *l,* drop one of those letters, when a termination is added that begins with a consonant: as, dull, dully, dulness; full, fully, fulness; will, wilful.

The words illness, shrillness, and stillness, retain the double *l,* agreeably to the general rule.

RULE VII.—Compound words are spelled in the same manner, as the simple words of which they are formed: as, household, horseman, forenoon, wherein, skylight, glasshouse, telltale, snowball, molehill.

EXCEPTIONS.

wherever	Christmas	martinmas
candlemas	lammas	michaelmas

Words that end with double *l* frequently omit one *l*, when they form parts of compound words: as,

Also	although	already	fulfil
almost	always	chilblain	welfare

In the present state of English orthography, it would be very difficult, if not impossible, to give precise directions respecting the single or double *l*, in compound words.* The same difficulty prevails with regard to words having the initials, *re, un, mis,* &c.—Uniformity in this point is much to be desired, though it can scarcely be expected. If the author were to hazard an opinion on the subject, it would be, that all compounds, except the preceding incorrigible words under the head exceptions, should be spelled with the double *l:* especially words in hill, mill, and those in which the *l* is preceded by *a* broad. In most instances, the sense or the sound, or both, appear to justify this rule; and the remainder might be defended on the principles of etymology and analogy. The opposite scheme, of making the *l* single, in compounds, would, in many cases, be highly improper: and there are no principles which would direct and warrant a middle course. This opinion derives support from Walker, author of the very judicious and highly useful Critical Pronouncing Dictionary.

---

* It is proper to observe, that the termination *ful*, in derivative words, is always spelled now with a single *l.* See page 188.

APPENDIX.

Exercises on various parts of the Spelling-book.*

Chapter 1.
Exercises on Part I.

Exercises on the first and second chapters.

Show the vowels in the words, if, ox, us, cat, hen, pig, dog, sun, egg, ink, and.

Show the vowels in, hand, tell, give, live, tongs, brush, crust.

Show the diphthongs in, head, said, guess, friend, been, flood, young.

Show the consonants in, skip, song, plum, grass, spell, thread, build.

Mention regularly the vowels, diphthongs, and consonants, in the following words: have, silk, gone, dead, touch, snuff, blood, breath, smell, guilt.

---

* The learner is to be exercised in each chapter, as soon as he has passed through the part of the spelling-book to which it relates.

Exercises on the second and third chapters.

Show the long and the short vowels in the following words: cake, she, hat, set, kind, home, pin, hop, mule, pure, cut, nut, grape, sand, here, best, mice, fish, cold, pond, fume, dust.

Show the long and the short diphthongs, in the following words: hail, day, head, clean, tree, tread, pie, buy, flood, road, snow, earth, learn, hue, few.

Exercises on the fourth and fifth chapters.

Show the middle and the broad vowels and diphthongs in the following words: star, heart, ball, straw, mouse, goose, owl, rook, lark, daw, moon, cloud.

Exercises on the seventh chapter.

Show the silent letters in the following words: crumb, neck, gnat, knee, walk, high, could, wrong, comb, sign, bright, sword.

Chapter 2.

Exercises on Part II.

Which are the accented syllables, in the following words? butter, deprive, quarrel, favour, deject, dismiss, thunder, resume, prepare, destructive, sausages, intervene, departure, distressful, perpetrate, carelessness, unconcern, contravene.

Show the short syllables in the following words: convey, impure, detect, resent, pervert, subsist, mannerly, fanciful, attractive, remaining.

Show the long syllables in these words: relieve, impute, finely, tallow, sincerely, oversee, violate.

Show the middle vowels and diphthongs, in the syllables of these words: barter, largely, heartless, reproof, discharge, untrue, gardening, faithfulness, foolery.

Show the broad vowels and diphthongs in the syllables of these words: falter, defraud, auburn, abound, wanted, mortar, purloin, bower, roundish, alderman, employer, appointment.

Show the mute vowels in the syllables of the following words: pickle, sable, mutton, token, hasten, treason, marble, possible, spectacle, fickleness, candlemas, sickening.

In the following words, point out those which are pronounced as one syllable, and those which are pronounced as two syllables: hoped, waited, bribed, played, wounded, basted, mourned, preached, toasted, stamped, smoked, heated, bended.

In the following words, mention regularly the accented syllables, the long and short syllables, the middle and broad vowels and diphthongs, and the silent vowels: stammer, offend, prattle, choked, mended, undone, export, retort, fairly, amount, afar, impart, proved, forsaken, fortitude, misinform, scenery, disconcert, exalted.

Chapter 3.

Exercises on the Rules for spelling, in Part III.

Chap. 19.

Section 1.

On the rules for dividing syllables.

Divide the following words into syllables, according to the rules at page 210.

RULE 1. Prefer, obey, reward, amuse, away, reason, linen, wagon, manage, imagine, ability.

Exact, examine, vixen, wagoner *.

RULE 2. Able, eagle, scruple, degree, reflect, secret, bestow, respect, despise, descend.—Posture, mustard, custom, distance, dismal, basket, muslin, hospital.

Abroad, ascend, astonish.

RULE 3. Summer, coffee, danger, certain, carpenter, advantage, entertain.

---

* The exercises in the smaller type, correspond to the exceptions in the same type under the rules.

Rule 4. Pastry, restraint, descry, esquire.—Display, distress, ostrich, industry.

Rule 5. Empty, hackney, chestnut, laughter, huckster, landscape, neighbour.

Rule 6. Feather, nephew, machine, orphan, mechanic, architect, arithmetic.

Rule 7. Real, riot, quiet, cruel, giant, idea, violet, gradual, punctual, industrious, mayor, flower, coward, shower, voyage.

Rule 8. Reader, teacher, mended, consider, builder, walker, coming, blessing, rolling, mistake, displease, mocker, tenderest.

Robber, running, fatted, forbidden.

Sentences, convinced, mincing, prancer, pacer, oranges, charged, stranger, ranging, partridges.

Smoker, rider, taking, shaven, wiped, bored, slavish, brutish, stupid, supposed, surprised.

Airy, hairy, steady, sooty, marshy, glossy, windy, misty, rainy, watery.

Rule 9. Almshouse, windmill, hartshorn, landlord, tradesman, posthorse, footstool.

Rule 10. Devotion, possession, contentious, delicious, confidential, brasier, cushion, ancient, soldier, surgeon, patiently.

Section 2.

On the rules respecting the double consonants, in primitive words.

Write or spell the following words according to the rules at page 216*.

RULE 1. Staff, stuff, puff, quill, till, fill, guess, bliss, moss, snuff, call, pass.

RULE 2. Dot, jug, man, fur, rib, pod, hum, pan.

Add, odd, buzz, bunn, inn, egg.

RULE 3. Proof, chief, meal, feet, school, boat, nourish, trouble, courage, meadow.

RULE 4. Canal, excel, distil, control, dispel, animal, daffodil, cathedral, parasol.

RULE 5. Clever, savage, proverb, exert, exist.

Clock, freckle, colic, cambric, hook.

RULE 6. Pebble, scuffle, smuggle, bottle, dazzle.

RULE 7. Penny, pretty, bonny, alley, volley.

Body, lily, money, honey, city, pity.

---

* The teacher is to pronounce these words, without the learner's seeing them at the time they are proposed for his exercise.

APPENDIX.

Rule 8. Ladder, hammer, garret, tippet, follow.

Proper, closet, shadow, spinet, consider.

Rule 9. Finish, mimic, timid, profit, vanity.

Attic, horrid, rabbit, skittish, necessity.

Rule 10. Accent, affect, efface, offend, offer.

Acute, acid, afar.

Rule 11. Amaze, catechism, elephant, epicure, moderate, paralytic, paradox.

Cattle, parrot, ammunition.

Section 3.

On the rules respecting derivative words, at page 220.

Rule 1. Write or spell the plural of the following nouns: sea, palace, college, eagle, bear, pound, shop, crab, dog, doll, sheriff, monarch.

1. Box, bass, dish, coach, sash, cross.

2 Negro, portico, mango, wo, torpedo.

3. Body, ruby, fancy, injury, apothecary. Valley, monkey, joy, play, journey.

4. Wife, leaf, self, knife, wolf, half.

5. Ox, penny, child, tooth, mouse, woman.

Rule 2. Join *ed* and *ing*, in a proper manner, to the following words: fade, hate, waste, desire, value, lodge, rejoice, believe.

Rule 3. Join *ness*, and *ly*, to the following words: late, like, rude, vile, fierce, polite.

APPENDIX.

RULE 4. Join *es, eth,* and *ed,* to the following words: try, deny, envy, reply, signify.

Join *ing* to the following words: fly, apply, deny, study, carry, empty.

RULE 5. Join *ed* and *ing* to the following words: wrap, plat, rub, prefer, regret, abhor.

Ravel, excel, equal, compel, quarrel.

RULE 6. Join *er, ed,* and *ing,* to the following words: dress, stroll, scoff, spell, kiss.

RULE 7. Write or spell the following words: skylark, busybody, foretell, windmill, downhill, uphill, wellwisher, farewell, holyday.

Section 4.

Promiscuous exercises on the rules and exceptions respecting derivative words.

Write or spell the plurals of the following nouns: umbrella, hero, army, history, dairy, life, sheaf, hoof, mouse, turkey.

Join *ed* and *ing* to the following words: change, inquire, enclose, move, continue, trifle, owe, die, disagree, hurry, fry, obey, employ, vex, sin, commit, visit, benefit, enter, inter, differ, defer, gallop, gossip, mention, quiet, quit, stuff, fill.

Join *able* to the following words: blame, value,

desire, agree, charge, service, manage, vary, justify, reason, excuse.

Join *er* to the following words: strange, free, oversee, write, inquire, saddle, cottage, die, cry, buy, visit, wagon, drum, begin, abhor, often, mill, jewel, commission.

Join *al* to the following words: refuse, remove, bury, deny, acquit, addition.

Join *ly* to the following words: complete, sole, whole, true, blue, servile, able, genteel.

Join *ly* and *ness* to the following words: idle, open, dim, sly, busy, cool, slothful, dull, stiff, cross, useless, harmless.

Join *ful* to the following words: plenty, fancy, duty, skill, success.

Join *y* to the following words: shade, ease, mud, sun, juice, noise, star, oil, meal.

Join *en* to the following words: forgive, rise, forgot, glad, wood, wool, deaf, stiff.

Join *ish* to the following words: late, rogue, hog, sot, prude, fop.

Join *ance* to the following words: ally, assure, vary, continue, remit, forbear.

Join *ment* to the following words: amuse, allot, judge, prefer, acknowledge.

Join *ous* to the following words: virtue, melody, poison, libel, vary.

APPENDIX.

To give variety to the exercises in spelling, and to prevent a dry and formal manner of performing this business, the learner should be frequently directed to spell, without seeing the words, the little sentences contained in the appropriate reading lessons, throughout the book. As these sentences are short, and contain no words that are not in the previous columns, they will probably form some of the most easy and agreeable spelling lessons, off the book, which the teacher can propose to his pupil.

When the learners have performed the exercises on the rules for spelling, they will, it is presumed, be prepared for entering, with advantage, on the study of the author's " Abridgment of his English Grammar." He hopes also that the latter chapters of promiscuous reading lessons, will qualify them for commencing the perusal of his " Introduction to the English Reader," or other books of a similar description. The transition, in both instances, will, he flatters himself, prove a natural and easy gradation.

THE END.

Recommendations *of this Work.*

"Mr. Murray has composed one of the best elementary books for children, in the English language."   *Critical Review.*

"An English Spelling-book from the author of the "English Grammar," will undoubtedly excite considerable expectation from those who have been in the habit of using the latter; and we doubt not that, in process of time, the spelling-book will have as many admirers, as the grammar has already obtained. We are glad to see that Mr. Murray has been careful in the right division of the syllables in his spelling; and that he has not followed the example of others, by introducing into his book a mass of irrelevant matter."   *Imperial Review.*

"Mr. Murray's elementary works have the sure merit of combining well-directed efforts to train the infant mind to virtue, with the best means of imparting instruction to it. In the spelling-book before us, this is particularly the case; and we can therefore safely recommend it as the best work of the kind which has lately fallen under our inspection."
     Anti-jacobin Review.

"In this book are several useful things, not commonly found in such works; for instance, Reading Lessons in Italic, Old English, and Manuscript Letters; explanations of the sounds of the letters, distinguishing the long and short sounds of the vowels, and the anomalous sounds of all; and finally, rules for spelling, very clearly and distinctly expressed. We have, on the whole, no doubt that teachers may find considerable advantage from adopting the use of this spelling-book."
     British Critic.

"Mr. Murray's successful exertions for the service of youth, have been so often before us, with applause, that we think it sufficient, on the present occasion, to announce the above publication; and to add, that it will not, in any manner, detract from the well-earned reputation of the author, in this department of literature."   *European Magazine.*

"We have, on more occasions than one, borne testimony to the great merit of Mr. Lindley Murray, as an able grammarian; and we are very glad to meet with him again in our annual survey. We have looked over his present book with considerable attention; and find in it much to commend. The volume is divided into three parts, &c.
Annual Review.

"This is a very neat and useful elementary book. The scale of instruction which the author has exhibited, is accurately graduated. The reading lessons are very appropriate, amusing, and useful. They are likewise free from the taint of the prevailing irreligion.—This author deserves much praise and encouragement, for the pains he has taken in purifying books of instruction: and the English Grammar, mentioned in the title of the present work, will establish his character as a writer in this important department of literature." *The Christian Observer.*

"This little book is singularly well adapted to answer the purpose for which it is intended; and must be an acceptable present to the teachers of English Youth. Mr. Murray, who has already displayed great skill in the department of instruction, will acquire additional reputation from this manual. The rules for spelling and pronunciation are good; and the Lessons, Examples, and Exercises, are judiciously chosen.—The book is entitled to our recommendation." *Monthly Review.*

MURRAY'S FIRST BOOK FOR CHILDREN.
The *Twentieth* edition.   Price 6d.

"This very improved primer is intended to prepare the learner for the author's English Spelling-book; and is particularly designed by him, to assist mothers, in the instruction of their young children.—This little volume is entitled to our recommendation." *Monthly Review.*

OF THE SAME BOOKSELLERS MAY BE HAD

The latest editions of Murray's English Grammar, and of his other publications, namely;

	s.	d.
1. A First Book for Children, 20th edition	0	6
2. An English Grammar, 47th edition	4	0
3. An Abridgment of the Grammar, 112th edition	1	0
4. English Exercises, 41st edition	2	6
5. A Key to the English Exercises, 20th edition	2	6
6. Introduction to the English Reader, 30th edition	3	0
7. The English Reader, 22nd edition	4	6
8. Sequel to the Reader, 7th edition	4	6
9. Introduction au Lecteur François, 6th edition	3	6
10. Lecteur François, 5th edition	5	0
11. Power of Religion on the Mind, 19th edition	5	0
12. The same work, on fine paper, with a Pica letter, 8vo, in boards	12	0
13. An English Grammar. In two volumes, octavo. Fine paper, and large type. Fifth edition, improved, in boards	1 1	0
14. A Selection from Bishop Horne's Commentary on the Psalms. Second edition	0 5	0
15. The Duty and Benefit of a Daily Perusal of the Holy Scriptures, in Families. Second edition, improved	0 1	0

⁎⁎⁎ These books may be properly considered as forming altogether a little code of important elementary instruction. Throughout the whole of them, the soundest principles of piety and virtue are happily blended with the rudiments of literature. And the pieces which they contain are mostly taken from some of our best classical writers. They may herefore, with perfect confidence, be put into the hands of young persons, as books which will, in no small degree, conduce to pure religion and morality, and to the acquisition of a correct and elegant style.

ALSO,

MEMOIRS of the LIFE and WRITINGS of LINDLEY MURRAY, in a Series of Letters, WRITTEN BY HIMSELF. With a PREFACE, and a CONTINUATION of the Memoirs, by ELIZABETH FRANK. In one volume, octavo, with a Portrait of the Author, and a Fac Simile of his Writing. Second edition, price, in boards, 9s.

(Thomas Wilson and Sons, High-Ousegate, York.)

www.ingramcontent.com/pod-product-compliance
Lightning Source LLC
Chambersburg PA
CBHW081325090426

42737CB00017B/3034